Lady Margaret Beaufort: Tudor Matriarch

A Tudor Times Insight

By Tudor Times

Published by Tudor Times Ltd

Tudor Times Insights

Tudor Times Insights are books collating articles from our website www.tudortimes.co.uk which is a repository for a wide variety of information about the Tudor and Stewart period 1485 – 1625. There you can find material on People, Places, Daily Life, Military & Warfare, Politics & Economics and Religion. The site has a Book Review section, with author interviews and a book club. It also features comprehensive family trees, and a 'What's On' event list with information about forthcoming activities relevant to the Tudors and Stewarts.

Titles in the Series

Profiles

Katherine Parr: Henry VIII's Sixth Queen

James IV: King of Scots

Lady Margaret Pole: Countess of Salisbury

Thomas Wolsey: Henry VIII's Cardinal

Marie of Guise: Regent of Scotland

Thomas Cromwell: Henry VIII's Chief Minister

Lady Penelope Devereux: Sir Philip Sidney's Muse

James V: Scotland's Renaissance King

Lady Katherine Grey: Tudor Prisoner

Sir William Cecil: Elizabeth I's Chief Minister

Lady Margaret Douglas: Countess of Lennox

Sir James Melville: Scottish Ambassador

Tudors & Stewarts 2015: A collection of 12 Profiles

People

Who's Who in Wolf Hall

Politics & Economy

Field of Cloth of Gold

Succession: The Tudor Problem

The Pilgrimage of Grace and Exeter Conspiracy

Contents

Preface

Margaret Beaufort could claim to be the matriarch of the Tudor dynasty. She transferred her precious Lancastrian blood to her son, Henry VII, and her descendants still sit on the British throne today.

Her life is a microcosm of the roles of women during the Wars of the Roses – married four times, all for political reasons, her husbands fought and died for both Lancaster and York. She served the Yorkist queens, whilst intriguing with the Lancastrian exiles to put her son, Henry, on the throne. Having achieved her ambition, Margaret went on to be one of the great patrons of education with the foundation of not one, but two, Colleges at Cambridge University.

This book contains Lady Margaret Beaufort's Life Story and additional articles about her, looking at different aspects of her life. Margaret was a great heiress, and her lands stretched across the Southern and Midland counties of England. Whilst the focus of the first two-thirds of her life were survival for herself and her son, and the successful pursuit of the English throne, she was also a cultivated and intelligent patron of the new printing press, translating works herself as well as commissioning them. Her Cambridge Colleges remain as a testament to her vision.

The material was first published on www.tudortimes.co.uk

Family Tree

Lady Margaret BEAUFORT
Countess of Richmond and Derby

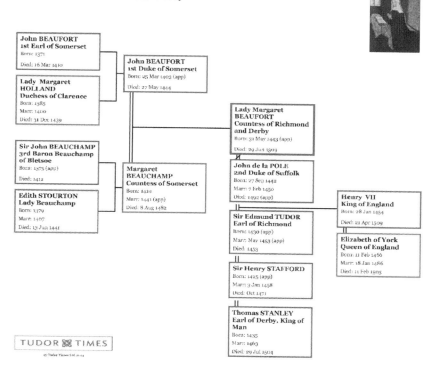

John BEAUFORT
1st Earl of Somerset
Born: 1371
Died: 16 Mar 1410

Lady Margaret HOLLAND
Duchess of Clarence
Born: 1385
Marr: 1400
Died: 31 Dec 1439

John BEAUFORT
1st Duke of Somerset
Born: 25 Mar 1403 (app)
Died: 27 May 1444

Sir John BEAUCHAMP
3rd Baron Beauchamp of Bletsoe
Born: 1375 (app)
Died: 1412

Edith STOURTON
Lady Beauchamp
Born: 1379
Marr: 1407
Died: 13 Jan 1441

Margaret BEAUCHAMP
Countess of Somerset
Born: 1410
Marr: 1441 (app)
Died: 8 Aug 1482

Lady Margaret BEAUFORT
Countess of Richmond and Derby
Born: 31 May 1443 (app)
Died: 29 Jun 1509

John de la POLE
2nd Duke of Suffolk
Born: 27 Sep 1442
Marr: 7 Feb 1450
Died: 1492 (app)

Sir Edmund TUDOR
Earl of Richmond
Born: 1430 (app)
Marr: May 1453 (app)
Died: 1453

Sir Henry STAFFORD
Born: 1425 (app)
Marr: 3 Jan 1458
Died: Oct 1471

Thomas STANLEY
Earl of Derby, King of Man
Born: 1435
Marr: 1463
Died: 29 Jul 1504

Henry VII
King of England
Born: 28 Jan 1454
Died: 21 Apr 1509

Elizabeth of York
Queen of England
Born: 11 Feb 1466
Marr: 18 Jan 1486
Died: 11 Feb 1503

Part 1: Margaret Beaufort's Life Story

Chapter 1: The Heiress

The Beaufort family was descended from John of Gaunt, third son of Edward III, via his third wife Katherine Swynford. John of Gaunt and Katherine's four children had all been born whilst he was married to his second wife and were thus illegitimate.

Following their parents' marriage in 1397, the children were legitimised by Act of Parliament. The Act permitted them all the rights of children born in wedlock, however their half-brother, Henry IV, excluded the ability to inherit the throne from their rights by Letters Patent. Letters Patent were not binding on the King's successors in the way an Act of Parliament was, but gave a strong indication that Henry IV, who had four sons of his own, did not see his half-siblings as potential heirs.

Despite any disappointment the Beauforts may have felt about this exclusion, they remained stalwart supporters of the Lancastrian kings, Henry IV, Henry V and Henry VI.

Lady Margaret Beaufort was the grand-daughter of the oldest Beaufort son, John, 2nd Earl of Somerset, and his wife, the great heiress, Lady Margaret Holland.

Margaret's great-uncle, Cardinal Henry Beaufort was one of Henry VI's most important councillors during that king's long minority, and her aunt, Joan Beaufort, was Queen of Scots. The power of Cardinal Beaufort was resented by the young Henry VI's uncle, Humphrey, Duke of Gloucester, and factions began to build around them.

In 1419, aged about 16, Lady Margaret's father, John, 3rd Earl of Somerset, together with his younger brother, Thomas, sailed for France as part of a new offensive in the Hundred Years' War. He was captured at the Battle of Bauge in March 1421 and spent 17 years as a prisoner. Various attempts to ransom him failed and it is perhaps unsurprising that on his release he was keen to make up for lost time in gathering wealth and support. His eventual ransom was huge - £24,000, compared with an annual income from his lands of less than £1,000.

Some four years after his release in 1438, John married Margaret Beauchamp of Bletsoe, the widowed Lady St John, already mother of seven children. Margaret Beauchamp, although not of particularly distinguished birth, was a considerable heiress, however Somerset's brother, Edmund, did far better in the marriage stakes when he managed to snag Eleanor, daughter of Richard Beauchamp, Earl of Warwick.

The new Countess of Somerset became pregnant almost immediately and Margaret was born on 31 May 1443.

In the period just before Margaret's birth the English crown had lost the vast majority of the French territories that were conquered during the reign of Henry V. The government was torn on the right action to take. The vast majority wanted to continue the wars, because, after all, war was what most of them had been born and trained for. However good leaders were lacking, money was short and the King himself, now of age, was far from being a warlike character.

Not long after Margaret's arrival, Somerset was appointed to lead a major expedition into France. Why he should have been selected, when his only military experience was the battle in which he had been captured, is a mystery. It was, perhaps, an attempt of the Beaufort faction at court to counter the influence of Richard, Duke of York. York, who was the next heir male after the King's uncles (none of whom had children), was a supporter of Gloucester against the Cardinal, and was the King's Lieutenant in Normandy.

Somerset's brief was designed to give him seniority everywhere in France except those parts where York was in control. Nevertheless, York felt slighted, and, since both men seem to have been touchy, relationships between the factions at court deteriorated. Somerset does not seem to have been eager to set out – understandable, given his previous experiences. He drove a hard bargain with the King's Council. His earldom was promoted to a dukedom, and he acquired new lands in anticipation of success.

Had Somerset been successful in France things might have turned out very differently both for himself and Henry VI, but he failed to achieve any lasting gains and there were concerns about his management of funds. Even Henry VI, that most pacific of Kings, was angry at the waste of money and men.

An investigation was held into Somerset's handling of the affair and some of his property was confiscated. The disgraced duke died shortly after his return, possibly by suicide, and was speedily buried at Wimborne Minster in Dorset.

The Beaufort inheritance, which had been granted *in tail male*, passed to Margaret's uncle Edmund, now 2nd Duke of Somerset. However, the lands that her grandmother, Lady Margaret Holland, held, could pass through the female line and therefore they became Margaret's inheritance. This made Margaret a significant landowner from an early age. The majority of her lands were in the south of England in Somerset Devon and Hampshire.

Chapter 2: Wardship and Wedding

The widowed Duchess of Somerset married for a third time, to Lionel, Lord Welles, and presented Margaret with three new half-siblings. During Margaret's childhood she lived with her mother, her St John half-siblings and her mother's new family, at Bletsoe Castle and, more frequently, at Maxey Castle in Northamptonshire. Her father's illegitimate daughter, Tacine, was also part of the household. It is evident from her later actions that Margaret was deeply attached to her St John and Welles relatives.

Little detail is known of Margaret's early education – her later scholastic leanings may have been apparent from an early age, or may have been the fruits of age and experience. We can assume she would have learnt to read in French and English, and probably to write in both languages. She would also have learnt the skills of managing a household, and, as she was an heiress, perhaps some basic land law. She certainly took a strong and direct interest in managing her estates in later life, as her mother had.

Before Duke John had left for France it had been agreed that, in the event of his death, the wardship of his daughter Margaret and his unborn child (the Duchess was pregnant at the time, but either miscarried or lost the child soon after birth) would remain in the hands of the Duchess. However, within a year of Margaret's birth, Henry VI granted the wardship and marriage of Margaret to his closest adviser, William de la Pole, Earl of Suffolk. Unusually, Margaret remained in the care of her mother, rather than being brought up in the household of her guardian.

The Earl of Suffolk was thoroughly unpopular, largely because he had negotiated the marriage of Henry VI to Marguerite of Anjou, in 1445, resulting in a peace treaty with France. In the long-run, this was probably the only sensible option; England could not support the financial burden of repeated attempts to win the French Crown, however, at the time the truce was considered weak at best and the action of a traitor at worst.

In early 1450, Suffolk was impeached. As part of the charge against him, it was alleged that he had designs on the throne - apparently planning to marry his son, John de la Pole, to Margaret in order to claim the throne in her right. However it seems unlikely that he had any such plan as he had actually already planned to marry his son John to a far greater heiress than Margaret - her distant cousin Anne Beauchamp, daughter and heiress of Henry Beauchamp, Duke of Warwick.

In the event, Anne Beauchamp died young and seven-year-old John was indeed married to six-year-old Margaret in 1449. These facts were used against Suffolk and he was disgraced and sentenced to banishment. Before he could reach France, his ship was captured in the English Channel, and he was unceremoniously executed, by supporters of his rival, Richard, Duke of York.

Margaret's marriage to John de la Pole was not to last. With Suffolk dead, Henry VI decided to transfer her wardship and marriage to his half-brothers, Edmund and Jasper Tudor. The Tudor brothers were the sons of Queen Catherine de Valois' second marriage to Owain Tudor, a gentleman of her household, and a descendant of the Welsh princes. This marriage was considered most unsuitable, and Queen Catherine was obliged to spend her subsequent life in retirement. By the early 1450s, however, Henry VI was showing a distinct interest in his mother's second family – perhaps worn out by the endless rivalry of his paternal relatives.

Although it was common practice for children to be pre-contracted to marry in their childhood, it was stipulated that they had to confirm the marriage when they reach the age of discretion which, for girls, was considered to be 12 and, for boys 14. The marriage could be repudiated at any time before it was completed. However, any decision not to ratify the marriage had to be evidenced by a public statement in front of witnesses, including a Bishop.

Margaret and her mother were summoned to court, with orders to attend the King on Shrove Tuesday, 14th February, 1453. In later years, Margaret retained a hazy memory of the occasion, but she interpreted it as a vision. She believed that she had been given a genuine choice as to whether to confirm her marriage to John de la Pole, or whether to agree to marry Edmund Tudor. Her nurse advised her to pray to St Nicholas for advice, and he appeared to her in the dress of a Bishop, and told her to choose Edmund. It is highly unlikely that she would have been given any choice in the matter at all and her memory of a vision may have been a hazy recollection of the Bishop who witnessed her denial of the marriage.

Margaret and her mother were still at court in April, and took part in the Garter ceremonies on 23rd April. On 12th May 1453, King Henry paid a hundred marks for clothes for her. As neither of the Tudor brothers had any female relatives to provide a home for Margaret, she almost certainly remained with her mother, until she was married to Edmund Tudor, now Earl of Richmond, on 1st November, 1455 at Bletsoe Castle.

Chapter 3: Marriage and Childbirth

Whilst childhood marriage was common, and twelve was the age of consent for a girl, by the mid-fifteenth century it was unusual, although not unprecedented, for marriages to be consummated before the girl reached fourteen. It was not thought to be immoral or criminal in the way we now perceive it, but early consummation was discouraged because the health and well-being of the girl were considered to be at risk.

Despite these risks, Edmund consummated the marriage. He was about eleven years older than his new bride, who was small and slight for her age. There is no direct evidence about Margaret's experience of marital intercourse – whether she was terrified and hurt, or whether she accepted it as a matter of course. She remained attached to the memory of Edmund for the rest of her life, so we can perhaps hope he was gentle and kind. She was certain, however, that early childbirth damaged her. Fifty years later, when her grand-daughter was to marry the King of Scots, she objected to the match being agreed before the girl was fourteen, lest her husband not *'wait'* and *'would thereby injure her and endanger her health.'*

Richmond's motive for proceeding to impregnate Margaret as quickly as possible is unlikely to have been lust, but was not particularly creditworthy. If an heiress died during her husband's lifetime and they had children, he would have a life interest in her lands – that is, he would enjoy the income of them. If they had no children, the lands would pass to her heirs. Since Edmund had little property of his own, the sooner

Margaret gave him a child, the better, especially given the escalating political crisis.

Six months before Margaret's marriage, her uncle, Edmund Beaufort, 2nd Duke of Somerset, had been killed at the 1st Battle of St Albans, which had resulted from the removal of Richard, Duke of York from the position of Protector that he had held during Henry VI's catatonic illness.

Somerset had been Henry VI and Queen Margaret's greatest supporter, and his death, together with that of several other nobles raised the stakes. His sons, and those of the dead Lord Clifford and Earl of Northumberland, wanted revenge. York did not, at this point, have the support, or perhaps the intention, to claim the Crown himself, and he swore allegiance to Henry again.

During York's first Protectorate, Richmond, and his brother, had both supported the Duke – they were as aware as the rest of Henry's nobles that the King was incompetent. However, as soon as York took up arms against their half-brother, they made their support for Henry clear.

By the end of the November, Margaret and Edmund were in South Wales, living at the Bishop's Palace at Llandyfai (Lamphey) in Pembrokeshire, not far from Pembroke Castle. Whilst Pembrokeshire was far from London, it was not far enough to avoid war. In South Wales, Richmond was acting as the King's lieutenant. He was besieged in Carmarthen Castle, by Sir Walter Devereux, and Sir William Herbert, supporters of the Duke of York. Having captured the castle in September, the men imprisoned Richmond within it for some weeks. He was released, but died at home on 1st November, 1456, his first wedding anniversary. The exact cause of death is not certain – his patchy attendance at court and Parliament may indicate long-term poor health, but, at the time, some accounts claimed he died of plague – a good catch-all term, not necessarily meaning Bubonic plague.

Margaret, widowed at thirteen, was seven months pregnant and far from her mother in Bedfordshire. She was also under the age of majority, and was still in the wardship of her brother-in-law, Jasper Tudor, Earl of Pembroke. She quickly left Llandyfai, and travelled to the far safer haven of his castle of Pembroke. It was there on 28th January 1457 that she gave birth to her only child, Henry. It is apparent from Margaret's later words that the birth was a traumatic event for her and she is probably right that it permanently damaged her fertility. Despite having two further husbands she never conceived again.

Chapter 4: Remarriage

Margaret was not to remain a widow for long. Within two months of the birth she travelled to the Duke of Buckingham's manor, near Newport in Gwent, with Jasper. There the Duke, Jasper and Margaret discussed the possibility of marriage to the Duke's second son, Henry Stafford. Why Jasper and Margaret's choice fell on Buckingham's son is not documented. Certainly, Buckingham was one of the most powerful nobles in England, and was a staunch Lancastrian.

A dispensation was granted for the marriage by the Bishop of Coventry on 6th April 1457. The dispensation was required because Margaret and Henry Stafford were second cousins, both great-grandchildren of John of Gaunt. This relationship is an illustration of the complexity of kinship and loyalty in the period of the Wars of the Roses. Whilst Buckingham, descended from Edward III via his fifth son and his Duchess, Anne Neville, grand-daughter of John of Gaunt, were Lancastrians, Duchess Anne was the sister of Cicely Neville, Duchess of

York. Their half-nephew, Ralph Neville, 2nd Earl of Westmorland, was a strong Lancastrian, whilst their brother, Richard, Earl of Salisbury, and Salisbury's son, Warwick, were York's strongest supporters.

Henry Stafford's age at the time of his wedding to Margaret is uncertain. His parents were married sometime before 1424, however, his mother was only ten in that year, so, even if her marriage were consummated as soon as she was twelve, Henry, the second son, could hardly have been born before 1428. If his mother bore her first child at fifteen, Henry was probably born around 1430, making him about thirteen years older than his bride. It is likely that the marriage took place in Warwickshire at Buckingham's home of Maxstoke, on 3rd January 1458.

Buckingham probably settled money on the couple, although it was not necessarily paid until after his death, but the majority of their income came from Margaret's own estates.

Margaret and Henry were married for 14 years but not much is known about their personal relationship or her life during this period. Her parents-in-law both mentioned her in their wills (calling her, as was customary, by her title of Countess of Richmond.) This suggest a happy marriage and the couple appear to have travelled between Margaret's estates regularly, hunting as they went. Their main homes seem to have been at Bourne, in Lincolnshire, and, later, Woking.

Margaret's father-in-law, the Duke of Buckingham, died fighting for Lancaster at the Battle of Northampton in 1460 and her step-father fell in the Lancastrian army at Towton in March 1461. Henry Stafford also fought for Lancaster at Towton. However after this most bloody battle, in which the army of Yorkists decimated the Lancastrians, Stafford, together with many of the Lancastrian lords, accepted the victorious Edward, son of the Duke of York, as King.

Edward IV, following this victory, pursued a course of reconciliation with leading Lancastrians, and Stafford was able to secure a pardon for both himself and Margaret. This action meant that Margaret's estates were not confiscated. Unfortunately, however, she was parted from her son (Henry's whereabouts between 1458 and 1461 is not known for certain, but, if the King did not grant his wardship elsewhere, and there is no record of his doing so, he would have remained with either Jasper or Margaret. Since Jasper was unmarried, he is unlikely to have taken charge of such a small child).

The wardship and marriage of the young Henry Tudor was granted by Edward IV to Sir William Herbert, along with his uncle Jasper's earldom of Pembroke. Sir William Herbert paid a thousand pounds for the wardship and marriage and it is likely that he envisaged marrying Henry to his own daughter, Maud, although she was his senior by six years, or possibly his second daughter, Katherine.

As noted previously, it was common for the children of nobles, whose fathers were deceased, to be granted as wards to people that the King wished to favour. Margaret's parting from Henry was therefore not unusual, although, of course, it was deeply upsetting. She was able to write to him and even visit him at Raglan Castle in South Wales where he spent most of his childhood.

Margaret's wider family, too, were largely reconciled to York, at least initially, with her cousin, Henry Beaufort, 3rd Duke of Somerset, being shown enormous favour and trust by Edward IV once he had submitted to the King. Unfortunately for Edward, this trust was misplaced. Somerset found it impossible to maintain allegiance to York. Whatever his reasons – loyalty to his father, genuine belief in the Lancastrian cause, or some unknown personal motivation - he defected after having sworn allegiance to Edward IV. Unfortunately for Somerset he was captured and executed after the Battle of Hexham in 1464 and his brothers also had their lands confiscated. This betrayal, as he saw it, by Somerset, left Edward IV much less conciliatory thereafter.

Somerset's mother, Duchess Eleanor, the widow of Duke Edmund, was imprisoned and treated harshly. This must have been hard for Margaret. She had known her aunt in childhood and Duchess Eleanor had lived for considerable periods with Margaret's own mother. Similarly, Margaret's brother-in-law, Jasper, remained the most prominent member of the Lancastrian party, although he was now a wanted man, slipping between Wales, Scotland, France and Brittany to drum up support for Lancaster.

At the same time, Margaret's new marital family, the Staffords, were drawing closer to York. Henry Stafford's nephew, now 2nd Duke of Buckingham, was married to Katherine Woodville, sister of the Queen, a match that is said to have disgusted the proud nobleman, as the Woodvilles were considered parvenu.

In 1466 Stafford and Margaret received a royal grant of the former Beaufort Manor in Woking, which had been confiscated from Henry, 3rd Duke of Somerset. This became one of Margaret's favourite homes, although the couple still continued to visit their other properties.

Margaret continued to write to her son, Henry, and in September 1467 she and Stafford crossed the Severn from Bristol to Chepstow, a trip which cost 10 shillings, en route to Raglan Castle where they stayed with the Herberts for a week.

In the following year Margaret sent a stream of messages to Henry when he was carried in Herbert's train to North Wales where he would have witnessed the destruction of Jasper's Lancastrian forces at Twt Hill, near Caernarfon, and the surrender of Harlech Castle following an eight year siege.

In December 1468 Margaret and Stafford entertained Edward IV at their hunting lodge in Brookwood, a couple of miles from Woking. So far as is known, this was the first occasion when Margaret actually met Edward IV in person.

Chapter 5: Widowed Again

This domestic peace was not to last. The Yorkists, having won a comprehensive victory at Towton, had begun to fall out amongst themselves. In particular, Edward's brother, George, Duke of Clarence, and his cousin, the Earl of Warwick, were unhappy with the level of reward they had received, and resented the promotion of Edward's in-laws, the Woodvilles.

Warwick and Clarence plotted against the King, and in 1469, broke out in open rebellion. Edward summoned his forces, including Sir William Herbert, Earl of Pembroke and guardian of Henry Tudor, and met the rebels at Edgecote Moor. Edward was defeated and captured. The victorious Warwick summarily executed Pembroke, and Queen Elizabeth Woodville's father and brother were given a quick trial at Warwick's castle of Kenilworth before being beheaded.

Henry Tudor, aged twelve, was, luckily, swiftly whisked away by Sir Richard Corbett, who took him to safety at Weobley, where he was cared for by Lord Ferrers, nephew-by-marriage of Herbert, and a Yorkist. Margaret was frantic with worry and sent a group of eight men to travel first to Raglan then to Weobley. She sent gifts to the household of Lord

Ferrers and pocket-money for Henry, in particular to buy him bows and arrows.

Margaret was keen to have the wardship of her son back in her own hands and on the 21st October 1469 at the Bell Inn on Fleet Street, London, Stafford's Council met with that of Earl William of Pembroke's widow, Anne Devereux, to try to reach an accommodation. Margaret also went to meet George of Clarence, who had been granted the lands of the honour of Richmond, which, if there had been no war, would have devolved on young Henry. No immediate agreement was reached, and, just at this delicate juncture, Edward IV was released by Warwick and Clarence. They had realised that there was no hope of replacing Edward with Clarence, and the internal Yorkist strife risked letting in the Lancastrians.

Henry Stafford, nervous that Margaret's activities would be taken as a sign of disloyalty, rushed to Edward's feet with presents.

The brutal and incestuous nature of the conflict between Lancaster and York is shown by the next outbreak of war, which again directly affected Margaret. In 1470 Sir Thomas Burgh of Gainsborough, Edward IV's Master of the Horse, quarrelled with Richard, 7th Lord Welles, Margaret's step-brother, and Welles' son, Sir Robert, attacked Gainsborough Hall.

Lord Welles was summoned to London, being promised a pardon if he appeared in front of the King. Following Towton (where his father, Lionel, Margaret's step-father was killed) Welles had sworn allegiance to Edward, and fought for the Yorkists at Hexham in 1464. It is possible, but unproven, that the skirmish with Burgh was in support of Warwick and Clarence. Despite Edward's promise, Welles was executed. Sir Robert Welles now began to raise troops against the King. Edward IV summoned Stafford to join his army, which he did, meeting the King at Stamford in Lincolnshire on 12th March 1471.

Sir Robert Welles' forces were then comprehensively overcome by the King's army at the Battle of Losecote Field. Stafford was obliged to inform Margaret's mother of the death of her stepson – although it is possible that Margaret Beauchamp did not mourn him too strenuously. After his father's death he had challenged her over their respective inheritance rights.

Despite these victories, all was not going well in the Yorkist world. Warwick and Clarence had decided to throw in their lot with Queen Marguerite of Anjou and by July 1470 Edward IV had been forced to flee as Henry VI was reinstated on his throne. Henry however, did not have the ability or the temperament to be a successful king (particularly after having been held prisoner in the Tower since 1465) and before long Edward IV returned to reclaim the throne.

In October 1470, as part of the wardship negotiations mentioned earlier, young Henry had been delivered to Jasper at Hereford. Now that the Lancastrians were back in power Jasper and Henry rode to London for the new parliament and Margaret and Henry were reunited. This was probably the last time Margaret was to see her son until the day after the Battle of Bosworth. On 20 October Margaret, together with her husband Stafford, brother-in-law Jasper, and son Henry, dined with Henry VI's Chamberlain, Richard Tunstall. It is alleged that this is the occasion on which Henry VI pointed to the young Henry and said that one day he should be king. Margaret and Henry were together for a couple of weeks mainly based at Woking with a visit to Guildford, Maidenhead and Henley.

On 11 November Henry and Jasper returned to Wales. Margaret again began negotiations with the Duke of Clarence to try to secure some lands for Henry Tudor, but the best that could be agreed was that Henry would succeed to the honour of Richmond on the death of Clarence. All of this became academic as on 14 March 1471 Edward IV arrived back in Yorkshire.

Margaret and Stafford were faced with almost an insurmountable problem as to which side they should support.

Events were moving fast. Margaret's cousin, the Duke of Somerset, as head of the Lancastrian forces was now in London supporting Henry VI. He visited Margaret at Woking on 24 March 1471 and stayed for four days with a retinue of some 40 men. His objective was to persuade Stafford to join the Lancastrian forces but Stafford would not commit himself.

Somerset was planning to join the other Lancastrian force from France that was due to land in the West Country led by Queen Marguerite and Edward of Westminster, Prince of Wales. Meanwhile Edward of York was marching south towards London. At some point Stafford had to make a decision as to whether to support Lancaster or York.

In the event he selected York. His reasons for doing so are unknown. Both his father and his elder brother had fought valiantly for Lancaster and he himself had done so in the past. Perhaps he was mindful that he had personally sworn allegiance to Edward or perhaps he believed that Edward had more chance of victory. Edward had certainly shown himself to be an extremely competent general, and overall, the Yorkists won more battles than the Lancastrians during the conflict.

Whatever the reasons for Stafford's choice, on 12 April he headed towards Edward's forces, arriving at Barnet with a small contingent of men. Before he left, Stafford made his will, naming Margaret as his executor. On 14 April Edward's Yorkist army defeated the Lancastrians under the Earl of Warwick. Stafford was seriously wounded. Meanwhile what was left of the Lancastrian army, reinforced by Queen Marguerite and the Prince of Wales troops, was aiming to join up with the Lancastrian army which had been recruited by Jasper Tudor in Wales and there was a race to reach the Severn crossing before the Yorkists caught up with them.

At Tewkesbury the two forces met, the Lancastrians still not with their full complement and the Yorkists exhausted from Barnet and a long march. The Yorkists won a resounding victory and Somerset and the other Lancastrian leaders were killed, even those who had reached the sanctuary of Tewkesbury Abbey.

Edward IV was now unchallenged King. Edward, Prince of Wales was dead, possibly on the battlefield but more likely killed in the presence of Edward and his brothers, Gloucester and Clarence. Henry VI also died in the Tower as soon as Edward reached London. He was almost certainly helped on his way although the reason for his death was given as *pure displeasure and melancholy*.

Stafford's decision to support Edward IV now paid off. Although after Towton Edward IV had shown himself to be in favour of reconciliation with Lancastrians, by now the changing fortunes of war and the increasing bloodiness of the conflict had brought the King's ruthless side to the fore.

Margaret was in a position to plead for her mother and her other Lancastrian relatives but she did not trust the King completely. During Henry VII's reign, Bernard Andre, his chronicler, recorded that Margaret wrote to Jasper and to Henry in Wales warning them not to accept a pardon from Edward IV. Margaret was no doubt concerned that had Henry been granted a pardon, he might well have gone the same way as Lord Welles and the young Edward, Prince of Wales.

Motivated by Margaret's warning or believing that there was no hope for the Lancastrian cause, Jasper and Henry escaped to France.

On 4 October 1471 Margaret was widowed again as Henry Stafford died of the wounds received at Barnet. He was buried at Pleshey.

Margaret was still only 28 years old. She had been married three times and widowed twice – losing one husband to Lancaster and one to York. Her very name was suspect and it was incumbent upon her to try to protect herself and her inheritance so far she could. She therefore chose to marry again with all speed.

Chapter 6: Yorkist Courtier

Margaret's choice for her fourth husband was Thomas, Lord Stanley. The Stanleys were an influential family, based in north-west England and north-east Wales, holding huge tracts of land in Cheshire and Lancashire. They were also hereditary Kings of Man. Margaret arranged her marriage to Thomas Stanley in some haste, not even waiting for the traditional year of widowhood to be completed. This suggests that there was no possibility whatsoever in her mind of her being pregnant.

The marriage between Stanley and Margaret was one of territorial ambition. Stanley had little or no influence in the southern counties and Margaret needed somebody to protect her and her lands. Stanley is remarkable for having negotiated the Wars of the Roses without ever committing himself or his troops to battle. He did however, serve Edward IV faithfully.

The marriage probably took place in Lancashire at the Stanley's principal residence at Knowsley early in June 1472. Although there was still an age gap between Margaret and her fourth husband, it was less than that between her and her previous husbands. Stanley was around 37 at the time of their marriage, widowed and with children by his first marriage to Lady Eleanor Neville, sister of Warwick the Kingmaker.

Margaret and Stanley travelled widely in the next few years amongst her lands and his. Her house at Woking was extended but she also spent time at his properties in the north including Knowsley and Latham. Stanley appears to have trusted his wife and relied upon her business sense evidenced by the reference to her, amongst others of his trusted advisers, of some of the regular land disputes that occurred between tenants,

The couple were frequently at court. Unlike others of the Yorkist nobility, Stanley seems to have had a good relationship with the Woodvilles. Stanley's son and heir by his first wife, George, Lord Strange, was married to Queen Elizabeth Woodville's niece.

Lady Margaret's place at court and good relationship with the King and Queen, was emphasised by her presence in November 1480 at the celebration of the birth of Bridget, the seventh child of Edward IV and Elizabeth Woodville. Margaret carried the baby to her christening.

This intimacy with the Queen was later to pay dividends.

Margaret's overriding desire was to provide for her son Henry. In May 1472, following the death of Stafford and prior to her marriage with Stanley, Margaret drew up a will which would have transferred her estates to Henry, on the assumption that by the time of her death he would be back in royal favour. It is easy to look back with hindsight and think that Margaret was planning all along for her son to become King, however it is probably more realistic to believe that she accepted that

Edward IV's dynasty was secure. He had two sons to follow him and was a popular King.

On 3 June 1482, in the presence of the King at Westminster, a document was drawn up intended to safeguard Henry's future. The first item was Stanley's promise not to interfere with the settlement of Margaret's estates made in her 1472 will. The second item dealt with the disposition of the estates that Margaret had inherited the previous month on the death of her mother, Margaret Beauchamp. Henry, referred to as 'Earl of Richmond' was to receive lands to the value of 600 marks a year upon certain conditions, the first of which was that he was to return from exile to *be in the grace and favour of the King's Highness*'. Edward IV confirmed this agreement by sealing the indenture.

In 1486 Stanley stated that at the time of this agreement Edward IV and Margaret had discussed the possibility of marriage between her son Henry and his elder daughter, Elizabeth of York. However Margaret's biographers, Jones and Underwood, dispute this. Their contention is that, had Edward IV considered a marriage to his daughter at that time, it would have necessitated a land grant to Henry to be made immediately, otherwise Elizabeth would have been married far beneath herself.

On balance it seems unlikely that Edward IV would have considered such a step. It's far more likely that Stanley was attempting to give Henry's accession to the throne some hint of justification by Edward IV. It was not long after this alleged discussion that Elizabeth of York was betrothed to the Dauphin of France.

Chapter 7: Reign of Richard III

On 9th April 1483, Edward IV died. He was only 40 years old. He had two sons, Edward, now Edward V, and Richard of Shrewsbury, Duke of York.

Edward V had been brought up largely at Ludlow Castle and the Marches of Wales. He was now brought towards London in the care of his maternal uncle, Anthony, Earl Rivers.

The King's party was met at Stony Stratford by his paternal uncle, Richard, Duke of Gloucester. Richard swore allegiance to Edward, but arrested his uncle and half-brother and sent them to Pontefract Castle in Yorkshire for safekeeping. They were executed without charge or trial on 25 June 1483

A protectorate was established under Richard, however within a few weeks he declared that all of the children of Edward IV and Elizabeth Woodville were illegitimate. He assumed the Crown as Richard III. Edward V and his younger brother were last seen in the Tower of London in the summer of 1483.

During this period neither Stanley nor Margaret appear to have made any objections to Richard's actions. In fact, they both appeared to be in high favour. The day prior to Richard's coronation he met with Margaret and Stanley with regard to debts owed to Margaret from the family of the Duke of Orleans, an overdue ransom from the French wars.

The next day, 4 July 1483, when Richard and his wife, Anne Neville, daughter of the Earl of Warwick, were crowned at Westminster Abbey,

Margaret carried the Queen's train. She also served the Queen at the coronation banquet, together with Katherine, Duchess of Norfolk, Richard III's maternal aunt.

In the aftermath of the coronation, Margaret attempted to come to an accommodation with Richard. Using Richard's ally, the Duke of Buckingham, who was also her nephew by marriage, the possibility of a marriage between Henry Tudor and a daughter of Edward IV was again mooted.

Despite this, it soon became apparent that Richard did not completely trust either Stanley or Margaret, perhaps because of their relationship with Elizabeth Woodville who had retreated to sanctuary at Westminster Abbey. Stanley's son, George, Lord Strange, was kept close by the King.

Richard III's usurpation of the throne led to widespread discontent among those who had been loyal to his brother Edward. Within weeks there were plots against him and it has been alleged that Margaret was part of an attempt to free Edward V from the Tower with a view to him being restored to the throne supported by Henry and Jasper. Henry would then be married to Edward V's sister Elizabeth of York. It is rather difficult to believe that Margaret would have risked everything for Edward V. In any event, the attempt was unsuccessful, and before long, Edward V disappeared from view.

Margaret had had a good relationship with Queen Elizabeth Woodville and this alliance now became the basis of negotiations to overthrow Richard. Surprisingly, no bar was put in place to messages passing between Margaret and Elizabeth Woodville at Westminster Abbey. The messenger was Margaret's physician, Lewis Caerleon. Simultaneously, Margaret was corresponding with Henry in Brittany via her servant Hugh Conway.

At the beginning of Richard's reign, the Duke of Buckingham was one of his chief supporters, however by the end of that first summer the two had fallen out. It is not clear why Buckingham deserted Richard. There are a number of theories, including that Buckingham was repelled by the murder of Edward V and his brother Richard, or that Buckingham had always intended to press his claims to the throne. He was descended from Thomas of Woodstock, fifth son of Edward III, and as such his claim, which was through the maternal line, was weaker than that of both Margaret and Richard.

Later, the Tudors would claim that Buckingham was rebelling in order to place Henry Tudor on the throne, however such an idea seems highly unlikely. Buckingham had received huge grants and marks of favour from Richard. Why would he risk that for an unknown exile?

On 24 September 1483 Buckingham wrote to Henry and invited him to join the rebellion, which was also supported by Edward V's half-brother, Thomas, Marquess of Dorset. and Sir Edward Woodville. Unsurprisingly he did not address Henry as the rightful King. Margaret was prominent in the plans for the rebellion, although again it is difficult to believe that she would have promoted anyone other than her son as King.

It may be that she was playing a long game and encouraged Buckingham to believe that he should claim the throne for himself, with the hope that he would either overreach himself and fail, resulting in his removal in his rebellion by Richard, or that if the rebellion were successful, Henry would be preferred by either the nobles or the Commons. It is certainly possible to believe that Margaret was so attached to her son that she believed everyone would follow him. Alternatively, Buckingham was attempting to fool Margaret into thinking that he would support Henry, whilst planning the rebellion for his own benefit.

Whatever Buckingham's plans, his rising, both that led by himself in South Wales, and that led by the Woodvilles and the Greys in Kent, was crushed. Buckingham did not have the support of his tenantry. He was betrayed by one of his own men and captured by the King.

Henry had raised a small fleet in Brittany and set sail for the south-west coast of England. On arrival he became suspicious that the men sent to greet him and inform him that Buckingham's rebellion had been successful were not genuine, and he turned away from the shore and sailed back to Brittany.

Margaret was now at risk. Her part in the rebellion was known, and it was only the fact that her husband had been completely unaware of her plans and had remained loyal to Richard that saved her and her lands. It's hard to believe that Stanley had no idea what was going on, however he remained sufficiently aloof from it to be able to claim complete innocence. Margaret was attainted in the Parliament of 1483 and her lands were granted to her husband. Although Margaret must have felt the blow of losing direct personal control, this was a far more lenient punishment than might have been meted out – although at this date no royal or noble women had been executed for treason, they had certainly been punished in unpleasant ways, by incarceration in either prisons or convents. Nevertheless, the punishment was as harsh as consistent with retaining Stanley's loyalty, a virtue of which Richard could not be certain.

Stanley was promoted to Lord Steward of the Household and Constable of England, in the hope of keeping him onside, however, Richard miscalculated. It is far more likely that Stanley refused to join Buckingham's rebellion because he resented Buckingham's influence in South Wales, rather than because he felt any loyalty to Richard.

Margaret's personal role in fomenting rebellion and negotiating with both Buckingham and the Woodvilles in a long-term plan to promote her son, indicate that her character was both steely and pragmatic. She was willing to achieve her goal for Henry by negotiation, as with Edward IV, by trickery, as with Buckingham, and by long-term planning, as with Elizabeth Woodville.

Chapter 8: The Invasion of 1485

Throughout 1484 and 1485 Margaret was in constant communication with Henry. The extent to which Stanley was involved is not certain. Both Stanley and his brother, William, were somewhat hamstrung by the fact that their sons were in Richard's control.

In early August, Henry Tudor and his uncle Jasper landed at Milford Sound in South Wales. They marched north through West Wales and throughout the period of their march they were in constant communication with the Stanley brothers.

Once he reached Cardigan, Henry wrote to the Stanleys, informing them that he intended to cross the River Severn into England at Shrewsbury. This suggests that he was fairly confident of Stanley support but they never gave unequivocal demonstrations of allegiance to Henry. Henry also sent his chaplain to Margaret at Lathom Castle to arrange a rendezvous.

When Henry reached Shrewsbury the gates were locked against him. The Mayor of Shrewsbury had sworn allegiance to Richard and said that he could not break that oath other than over his dead body. He was soon in a cleft stick, however, as one of William Stanley's retainers, Roland Warburton, sent a message to Shrewsbury requiring the town to allow Henry to pass. Shrewsbury was heavily dependent on Stanley favour so the Mayor dealt with his promise by lying down on the road and permitting Henry's horse to step over him. Henry and his men passed peacefully through Shrewsbury, carefully paying for all of their goods and refraining from any molestation of non-combatants. Previous Lancastrian armies had had a bad name for the treatment of civilians.

Meanwhile Richard had sent orders to the Stanley brothers to raise men to support him. Both Stanleys raised considerable contingents and marched towards the Midlands. During their march they were careful neither to meet with Henry's army nor with Richard's. This would keep their options open.

Henry seems to have been fairly certain of the Stanleys support for him. There were at least two secret meetings with the brothers en route the Bosworth, although Lord Strange was still being held by Richard as hostage.

Stanley and his army left Lathom on 15 August, heading for Newcastle-under-Lyme in Staffordshire, reaching the town of Lichfield on 17 August. It seems that Stanley had put in a good word for Henry who arrived in Lichfield the day after he had left. Lichfield offered no resistance and neither did Tamworth. On 20 August Stanley sent a message to Henry that Richard's army was close by and that battle could be expected within a few days.

The nobility of England were rapidly losing interest in fighting for rival Kings. Of the nearly 60 peers of the realm in 1485, only half made any attempt to join Richard and only six were definitely part of his army.

The night before the battle it is likely that Henry met with his stepfather who no doubt had many messages of love and support from

Margaret. Nevertheless, the Stanleys' armies did not join those of Henry. Instead they stayed somewhat aloof, although four of Stanley's best knights and retainers were sent into Henry's vanguard

The Battle of Bosworth was not well recorded at the time and there are many different theories as to exactly what took place, some of which are now becoming clearer following extensive and continuing excavations and archaeological investigations at the site. What is clear is that the Stanleys waited and did not commit themselves to battle.

Before battle was joined Richard, suspicious that the Stanleys intended to join with Henry, ordered the execution of Lord Strange. The orders were not carried out.

The climax of the battle came when Henry apparently rode towards Sir William Stanley to request his support. Seeing Henry separated from the main body of his troops, Richard charged. Spotting the opportunity created by Richard being separated from the main body of his army, William Stanley led his troops in support of Henry. In the ensuing melee, a number of Henry supporters, including his standard-bearer, Sir William Brandon, were killed and so was King Richard.

Chapter 9: My Lady, the King's Mother

Henry was crowned in an impromptu ceremony on the battlefield. He rode south to London arriving in the capital by 7 September and took up residence at Baynard's Castle. Henry then left the capital to visit his mother at Woking, where she had raced immediately upon hearing the news of the victory at Bosworth. He was there for at least a fortnight and during this period he showed his gratitude and affection for Margaret, now aged 41, by making extensive grants to her.

Margaret was granted the house of Coldharbour in London, overlooking the Thames and she was also assigned various noble wards - guardianship being a very lucrative business in the 15th century. Henry had promised to marry Elizabeth of York, making a solemn oath in Vannes Cathedral that, should he be successful in his conquest, he would marry the Yorkist heiress. Elizabeth, together with her younger sisters and cousin, Lady Margaret Plantagenet, had been at Sheriff Hutton, one of Richard's Yorkshire castles, at the time of the Battle of Bosworth. These royal ladies were now consigned to the care of Margaret.

She was also granted the wardship of Edward Stafford, Duke of Buckingham, son of the executed Duke Henry. The reason for this grant was probably threefold: first, Buckingham was the wealthiest nobleman in England, and therefore the use of his lands during his minority would be of substantial benefit to Margaret: second, he was Margaret's great-nephew by marriage as well as her second cousin and thus a family connection; third, he had a viable claim to the throne and would require careful watching – a job that Henry could only entrust to his mother.

Margaret's husband Stanley received many of the spoils of the battlefield, including Richard's tapestries, which were sent to Knowsley. Margaret received Richard's Book of Hours. She also took into her household a number of the former King's servants and retainers, suggesting that there was a policy from the outset of the new reign to seek reconciliation.

For kingship to be completed in the 15th century, coronation was required. Henry's took place on 30 October 1485. An overjoyed Margaret is recorded as weeping with joy during the ceremony.

Henry VII's first parliament, which was not held until after the coronation lest there be any hint that Henry owed his crown to it, reconfirmed the legitimacy of the Beauforts, without that embarrassing edition of the clause excluding them from the crown. Henry did not dwell on his genealogical claims but rested his rightful kingship largely on his victory at Bosworth, which was seen to be justification at the hands of God himself.

Strictly speaking Henry's claim to the crown was weak. If female inheritance were permitted, as seems to have been generally accepted, then the legitimate heir was Elizabeth of York. If only inheritance through the male line were permitted, Henry had no claim at all. If Elizabeth's claims and those of the remainder of the York family were ignored, then Margaret herself should have been Queen.

It is not known whether Margaret ever considered herself as a realistic claimant to the throne. Although the principle of female inheritance was accepted, it is unlikely that people would have fought for a female claimant when a man was available. Nevertheless, Margaret almost immediately adopted semi-regal status. She was referred to throughout Henry's reign as '*my lady, the King's mother*' as well as by her titles of Countess of Richmond and Derby. Around the end of the century, she even took to signing her documents Margaret R, rather than the more usual noble style which would have been M Richmond. The '*R*' being ambiguous as it could have stood for Richmond or for Regina.

Similarly to a Queen, Margaret was granted by Parliament the status of a femme sole that is, she was able to manage her affairs as though she were either a single woman or a widow rather than a wife. Margaret was also permitted to retain men in livery, a licence not granted to any other woman.

Margaret was treated with almost the same regal status as her new daughter-in-law, Elizabeth of York, whom Henry married in January 1486. At Elizabeth's coronation, Margaret and Henry watched from a gallery, the usual practice of the King observing his wife's coronation, if it took place at a different time from his own. The following day Margaret sat at the Queen's right-hand as Elizabeth dined in state.

In 1487 she was recorded as wearing mantles and robes and a coronet indicating royal status and in 1488 when she and Elizabeth were invested as Ladies of the Order of the Garter – the last women to be so honoured before the 20th century – the two ladies wore the same Garter robes of red furred with miniver and woven with golden letters.

As well as the frequent use of her Beaufort portcullis badge in Henry VII's propaganda offensive, Margaret herself used the Royal fleur-de-lis. She too, had a cloth of estate. Of course, this lauding of the King's mother was not entirely new. Edward IV had treated his mother Cicely, Duchess of York similarly. Duchess Cicely tended to refer to herself as 'Queen by rights'. Margaret was never declared Queen by rights, yet the implication hung in the air.

Throughout the 1480s and 1490s Margaret was frequently with the King and Queen. In 1488 her Beaufort family was honoured when Edmund the last duke, Margaret's cousin, and his brother, John, were given a ceremonial reburial in Tewkesbury Abbey. Another Beaufort relative, the illegitimate Charles Somerset, was brought into royal favour.

Margaret was at Windsor in 1492 with Henry to oversee works to St George's Chapel and made a personal contribution of a hundred marks to the costs. In 1496 the King, the Queen and Margaret toured her estates in Dorset at Canford, Poole and Corfe where they stayed for a while on 30 July 1496. Corfe was an important part of the Beaufort inheritance and had been extensively improved and repaired by Margaret in 1488. The royal progress of 1496 also allowed a visit to Wimborne Minster, where Margaret's parents lay. She made an offering at their tombs. This visit to Margaret's estates was followed up by visits to the east of the country.

All three travelled east to be entertained at Castle Hedingham in Essex, by the Earl of Oxford, to whom Henry owed his victory at Bosworth, moving on to Bury St Edmunds, Thetford, Norwich, Walsingham and King's Lynn. By early September they reached Cambridge and then travelled through Huntington and Peterborough before arriving at Margaret's main residence outside London, Collyweston, on 7 September.

Margaret had lodgings assigned to her at all the royal palaces. At Woodstock, her chambers were linked to the Kings by means of a common withdrawing chamber. Apparently they often passed the evenings playing cards or chess together. Similarly in the Tower of London which was still in use as a royal palace, Margaret's rooms were next to the King's own bed chamber and council chamber.

Chapter 10: Cares of State

In 1492 Henry prepared to invade France. Margaret made significant contributions to the campaign – in the shape of a gift of £666 and a substantial supply of grain. Part of the justification for the invasion of France was the debt owed to Margaret for the ransom of the Duke of Orleans. In support of her claim, Margaret was permitted to use the Royal Secretariat. Henry and Margaret, living up to their later reputations for avarice, made a great deal of this debt, exaggerating the amount outstanding.

Margaret's first biographer, one might say hagiographer, Bishop Fisher, claimed that Margaret was constantly in tears for, at times of joy, she was always aware that the wheel of fortune could turn. This picture of a constantly weeping saint is hardly attractive to modern eyes but it was standard 16th century praise of pious women.

Whether or not Margaret cried frequently, she was certainly aware that fortunes could change very rapidly. The first twelve years of Henry VII's reign were troubled by frequent Yorkist insurrections. The first, led largely by John de la Pole, Earl of Lincoln, son of the man who as a child had been Margaret's first husband, had the aim of placing the pretender Lambert Simnel on the throne – presumably Lincoln intended to have him removed him as soon as the Yorkists were victorious. The rebellion was defeated at the Battle of Stoke in 1487.

A second, more serious, insurrection involved the use of another pretender, Perkin Warbeck, who claimed to be the younger of the Princes in the Tower. Family unity broke down as Sir William Stanley, perhaps believing that Warbeck was who he claimed to be, joined the conspiracy. Although William Stanley was executed, this does not seem to have affected Henry's relationship with his stepfather.

Thomas Stanley had been created Earl of Derby and was one of Henry's senior councillors. Nevertheless, it appears that both Henry and Margaret were unimpressed by Derby's minimal efforts at Bosworth and in 1504 Margaret took a vow of chastity and separated her household from his, although there was no open breach.

At the time, there were different views of the level of influence Margaret held. One contemporary commentator suggested that although Henry honoured his mother he didn't actually pay much attention to her advice. Others believed that she had a strong influence over him. She certainly played a more prominent role in advising the King than women had done since the days of the Angevin Queens in the 11th century.

This influence is demonstrated in her protection of Henry's sister-in-law, Cicely of York, Lady Welles, when, after the death of Margaret's half-brother Lord Welles, Cicely made a marriage that Henry heartily disapproved of. Despite being banished from court, Cicely was allowed to stay with Margaret at Collyweston.

Margaret and her Council were often given consent by the King to examine complaints and redress grievances. There are a number of instances in the late 1490s and early 1500s of men brought before Margaret's court for investigation. Unlike most courts of leading nobles, her powers extended beyond jurisdiction within her own lands. It even appears that she may have had a specific commission as in the 1520s when a petition was drawn up against the Duke of Richmond's Council of the North, Lord Darcy wrote that

'the... commission that my Lady the king's grandam had, was tried and appeared greatly to the king's disadvantage in stopping of the many lawful processes in course of his laws at Westminster Hall'.

It appears that Margaret was the only magnate Henry VII completely trusted. Margaret's power gave weight to the idea that a 'femme sole' could be appointed as a Justice of the Peace. In the early 17th century in a debate at Lincolns Inn on the validity of women as Justices, the King's Attorney declared that he had seen judgements made by her in that capacity.

In 1503, Margaret's power as King's deputy in the Midlands was very clearly shown in her arbitration between the town and University of Cambridge. The two sides were forever arguing and Margaret was now empowered to settle the matter. The parties selected arbitrators and she presided over a number of informal sessions to try to resolve the issues.

In May 1503 Margaret and her Council presided over the implementation of a complex agreement and the creation of rules for arbitrating any further disputes. Margaret herself was given power to deal with any further problems.

Margaret and Henry did not always agree. In 1503 he took her palace of Woking from her - substituting it with a life interest in Hunsdon, Hertfordshire, a step which Margaret obviously resented. On the King's death she took immediate steps to recover Woking.

Chapter 11: Matriarch

One of Margaret's roles at court was as custodian of royal etiquette and protocol. Her regulations on the correct manner in which a royal lady should prepare for childbirth were followed by her daughter-in-law, Elizabeth of York, and those wives of Henry VIII who bore children, as well as by her great-granddaughter Mary I, when she believed herself pregnant.

These regulations were soon required as Margaret became a grandmother within a very short space of time after her son's marriage. Her first grandchild was born, perhaps prematurely, in September 1486, and to the delight of everyone, proved to be a prince. Arthur, as he was named in homage to Henry VII's claimed descent from King Arthur, was soon followed by others.

In 1498 Margaret bought gold brooches for two of them, Princess Margaret (who was her goddaughter as well as her namesake) and Henry, Duke of York.

That Henry and Margaret enjoyed a close emotional bond cannot be denied. Their letters to each other are very much more affectionate than is common during the period. On his birthday in 1501 Margaret wrote *'this day of St Anne's that I did bring unto this world my good and gracious prince, king and only beloved son'.*

Nevertheless Margaret was not the only woman in Henry's life. He quickly became deeply attached to Elizabeth of York – the level of affection showed by Henry to Margaret, to Elizabeth and to his daughter Margaret suggests that, far from being the chilly presence he is often portrayed as, he was actually a man of warm personal emotions.

Early in 1501 was the zenith of Henry VII's reign. At that time he had three living sons, Arthur, Prince of Wales, Henry, Duke of York and Edmund, Duke of Somerset, as well as two living daughters, Margaret and Mary. He had agreed marriages between his two eldest children, Arthur to Princess Katharine of Aragon and Margaret to James IV, King of Scots.

Margaret took a considerable level of interest in the negotiations around these matches, although one aspect of her involvement was to discourage the match between Princess Margaret and James of Scotland on the basis that the Princess was too young to consummate the marriage. Presumably remembering her own experiences as a bride of twelve, Margaret did not wish her granddaughter to be exposed to the same dangers.

Margaret attended the wedding of Arthur and Katharine, sitting with Henry and Elizabeth in a small room overlooking the choir of St Paul's Cathedral whilst the marriage was solemnised. Her palace at

Coldharbour was extensively refurbished with the sum of 1000 marks being spent on cloth of gold and other elaborate provisions for the young couple to be entertained there following their marriage.

When Princess Margaret was eventually married to James IV of Scotland in 1503, it was from Margaret's home at Collyweston that she departed. Margaret noted the arrival of the royal party on 5 July in her Book of Hours. The court remained at Collyweston for three weeks with Margaret overseeing the lavish entertainment. Another important political event to occur at Collyweston was the marriage of Elizabeth, daughter of Margaret's half-brother, Oliver St John, to Gerald Fitzgerald, Earl of Kildare. Kildare, who had been a Yorkist supporter, was now appointed Henry's Treasurer in Ireland.

This marriage reflects the fact that, although Henry VII was undoubtedly Margaret's main focus, she was also deeply attached to her half siblings, and arranged advantageous marriages for many of them. It is contended by her biographers Jones and Underwood, that the marriage of Sir Richard Pole, her half nephew, to Lady Margaret Plantagenet, daughter of the Duke of Clarence, was the result of Margaret's influence. Similarly, the marriage of Elizabeth of York's sister Cicely to Margaret's half-brother, Viscount Welles, may also be seen as occurring to please Margaret.

Other interpretations of these events are that Henry VII had a deliberate policy of marrying Yorkist women to Lancastrian men and that as the Richard Pole was not of particularly exalted birth, this was quite a safe match.

Chapter 12: The End of an Era

Nevertheless, as Margaret always feared, good times cannot last forever. First, Prince Edmund died in 1500, then Arthur, within five months of his marriage, died in April 1502. Queen Elizabeth, in a bid to restock the royal nursery, died in childbirth in February 1503. Margaret, in her role of keeper of royal precedent, drew up the ordinances of the Queen's elaborate funeral. Later in the year there was a further thinning of the ranks at the English court as Princess Margaret left for Scotland.

In 1504 Margaret herself was widowed. We cannot infer anything about her marriage to Stanley, as there are no personal records to give any indication of their feelings for each other. One clue may be that the inauguration date of St John's College, founded by Margaret, and the annual Requiem Mass she required to be held at Wimborne Minster were the date of his death. The marriage had lasted for over 30 years and Stanley had protected her from the most serious consequences that could have flowed from her involvement in Buckingham's rebellion in 1483. During the last few years of their marriage they had been leading more or less separate lives after Margaret took a vow of celibacy.

A new menace appeared on the horizon to harass the King and, presumably, his mother. The brother of the late Earl of Lincoln, Edmund de la Pole, was now claiming the throne. In recognition of his Yorkist ancestry he was referred to as the White Rose.

In this matter, Henry was able to gain the upper hand when de la Pole was returned from his safe haven in Burgundy. In 1506, the Duke of Burgundy, Philip of Austria, together with his wife, Juana, Queen of Castile, had been shipwrecked in England. The couple had been sumptuously entertained, with Margaret involved in all the festivities.

Henry proved reluctant to let the stranded pair re-embark until Philip's father, the Emperor Maximilian, had agreed to return Edmund de la Pole. Maximilian required that Henry promise to spare Edmund's life, and Henry kept his word.

Towards the end of 1506, Henry, who had grieved for the loss of his wife sincerely, was considering taking a new wife. Henry's various marriage plans did not come to fruition – he does not seem to have prosecuted the matter with any great vigour and his reign descended into a time of darkness, increasing suspicion, and financial exactions which, now that men had forgotten the bloodier years of the wars, seemed tyrannical.

On a brighter note, in June 1507 Margaret attended court to watch a tournament in which her grandson Henry took part. She gave him the saddle and harness for his horse the following year as a gift when he proved capable at the game of *'running the ring'*.

During the years of the new century, Margaret was heavily involved in the development of her charitable schemes, in particular the foundation of Christ's Church College, Cambridge.

Henry VII was beginning to ail. When the he fell ill in 1508 Margaret returned to her home in Coldharbour from which she frequently journeyed down to his favourite palace of Richmond to visit him. In April 1509, the King died. He was just past 52 while Margaret herself was 65.

At the King's funeral in May 1509, largely arranged by Margaret, she took precedence over all the ladies present. She was also the chief executor of his will.

Following her grandson's coronation, Margaret moved to lodgings at Westminster. Technically Henry VIII, being not yet 18, was still a minor and Margaret was involved in the Council formed to manage the government. However she had been ailing since the beginning of the year and now she fell seriously ill. The immediate cause of her illness was attributed to eating a cygnet. She was given *'waters and powders'* but she did not rally and died on 29 June 1509.

Accounts of her death include two vignettes that reflect her character. Bishop Fisher, taking the religious perspective, recalled that when the last rites were performed, she *'with all her heart and soul she raised her body... And confessed a surety that in that sacrament was contained Christ Jesus the son of God, who died for wretched sinners upon the cross, in whom wholly she put her trust and confidence'*. Reginald Pole on the other hand, grandson of her half-brother, said that while she was dying Margaret had recommended that Fisher watch over Henry VIII carefully, lest *'he turn his face from God'*.

Margaret had made her will on 6 June 1508 and added further instructions in early 1509. She had chosen to be buried in Westminster Abbey in the Lady Chapel founded by Henry VII. On 3 July her body was moved to the Abbey where it lay in state until it was transferred into the Lady Chapel on the ninth of the month.

A contract for the construction of her tomb was entered into by her grandson Henry VIII on 23 November 1511. The work was performed by the Italian sculptor Pietro Torregiano who had also been commissioned to complete the tombs of Henry VII and Elizabeth of York.

An epitaph for the monument was composed by the humanist Erasmus. She is surrounded in death with the symbols of her ancestors, the Yale of Kendal and the Beaufort portcullis along the tomb, together with the arms of John, Duke of Somerset, Beauchamp of Bletsoe, Edmund Tudor, Earl of Richmond, Thomas Stanley, Earl of Derby, Henry V and Katherine of Valois, Henry VII, Elizabeth of York, her grandson Henry VIII and his wife Katharine of Aragon, and her grandson Arthur, Prince of Wales. The sermon preached at her month mind (a service held a month after the death) on 29 July 1509 was delivered by Bishop John Fisher who had been closely associated with Margaret in her various charitable endeavours. As with most funeral orations it concentrated on the departed's positive characteristics.

'All England for her death had cause of weeping. The poor creatures that were wont to receive her alms, to whom she was always piteous and merciful; the students of both universities, to whom she was as a mother; all the learned of England, to whom she was a [patron]; all the virtuous and devout persons, to whom she was a loving sister; all the good religious men and women whom she was so often wont to visit in comfort; all good priests and clerks, to whom she was a true defender; all the noble men and women, to whom she was a mirror an example of honour; all the common people of this realm, the whom she was in their causes, mediatrix and took right great displeasure for them; and generally the whole realm had cause to complain and to mourn her death.'

Conclusion

Lady Margaret Beaufort, from an inauspicious beginning as the daughter of a disgraced man who may have committed suicide, wove her way skilfully across the treacherous ground of the Wars of the Roses. She achieved what might have seemed almost impossible at the birth of her son in 1457 – his recognition as King, despite his rather tenuous claim to the throne and his successful passing on of the crown to her grandson, Henry VIII. Without Margaret's constant efforts it is unlikely that the Tudor dynasty would ever have been established.

Part 2: Aspects of Margaret Beaufort's Life

Chapter 13: Character and Interests

Character

After an interval of 500 years it is not easy to gauge anyone's character. Lady Margaret Beaufort, however, left more records than most people of her time and it is possible to glean an understanding of her life and outlook.

There have always been two schools of thought about Margaret - one has seen her as the great example of pious and devoted late mediaeval noblesse oblige, and the other as the scheming and ruthless power behind Henry VII's throne.

It is possible to see that elements of both of these characterisations may be true. Margaret was brought up in a hard school – the Wars of the Roses became increasingly violent, vengeful and bloodthirsty over time, with both sides indulging in acts of murderous retribution as sons sought to avenge fathers and brothers. It can hardly be surprising if Margaret used whatever power she had to protect her son and herself.

We cannot know whether Margaret's negotiations with Edward IV to bring about a reconciliation with her son in 1482 were genuinely prompted by a desire for peace and perhaps acceptance of the Yorkists as victors in the Civil Wars – at that time Edward IV had two living sons and numerous daughters. Margaret is unlikely to have thought that Henry would be considered a sufficiently strong candidate to displace him.

With the usurpation of Richard III in 1483, however, Margaret shows herself as a shrewd and quick thinking strategist. According to Polydore Vergil, *'being a wise woman'* she quickly grasped that Richard's deposition of his nephew, Edward V, and the disappearance of the twelve-year old King and his brother had alienated a huge swathe of York's support. She acted to capitalise on that as quickly as she could, working with the Dowager Queen, Elizabeth Woodville, to arrange a marriage between Henry and Elizabeth of York, and also conspiring with the Duke of Buckingham.

One of the accusations against Margaret is that she led Henry, 2nd Duke of Buckingham (1455 – 1483) into rebellion against Richard III. Margaret knew Buckingham well. He was the nephew of her second husband, Henry Stafford. Orphaned after Towton, he became a ward of Edward IV. Edward, in his desire for reconciliation with Lancastrians, married the boy to his sister-in-law, Katherine Woodville. Despite having lost his father and grandfather in the Lancastrian cause, Buckingham grew up to support first Edward, then Richard III. During his adolescence, Buckingham visited Margaret and Stafford, even spending Christmas with them at Woking in 1469, suggesting a good family relationship.

Buckingham was, initially, Richard's chief supporter. He was rewarded with vast lands (the return of part of the de Bohun inheritance that he claimed had been illegally incorporated into the Crown by Edward IV, rather than devolved to him in line with common law on the death of Henry VI) and an extension of his authority in Wales. Suddenly, in the late summer of 1483, he rebelled.

The question has always been, why? Buckingham had a very respectable claim of his own to the throne, but why press it then? It has been suggested that he was horrified by the murder of Edward V and Richard, Duke of York. Whilst there is controversy over whether Richard III was responsible for their deaths, by the summer of 1483, concerns about the fate of the children had been raised, and they were not produced to refute rumours. On the other hand, Buckingham himself has been fingered as a possible culprit, either advising Richard to dispatch them or undertaking it himself, although most historians agree that he is unlikely to have been able to affect the murder of the boys without Richard's knowledge.

The theory is that Margaret, via Dr John Morton, Bishop of Ely, encouraged Buckingham into raising an army, perhaps tempting him with the idea that he should be King himself, rather than that he should raise an army for her son. It certainly beggars belief that Buckingham would rebel on behalf of Henry Tudor – an unknown exile. He is far more likely to have been trying to persuade Margaret to support his own cause and ended up being double-crossed.

Morton, who had objected to Richard III's usurpation, was imprisoned in Brecknock Castle, Buckingham's stronghold in South Wales, and it was apparently whilst there that he suborned Buckingham. Messages passed between the anti-Richard Yorkists, and the Lancastrians, including Margaret, culminating in the failed rebellion of 1483, which resulted in Buckingham's execution. If Margaret encouraged Buckingham into rebellion, he has to take ultimate responsibility for his own actions – had he been successful, it is unlikely he would have been keen to share power with Margaret or her son.

Buckingham's son, Edward, 3rd Duke, became Margaret's ward, but he, too lost his head in 1521, accused of plotting against Margaret's grand-son, Henry VIII.

The far more serious charge, that Margaret was involved in the death of Edward V and his brother, was first mooted in the early seventeenth century by Sir George Buck, who may lay claim to being the first Ricardian. He accused her of attempting to murder the boys by sorcery or poison. His source for this (an *ancient manuscript*) has not yet been found. Leaving aside sorcery (which even if it were practised, seems unlikely to be efficacious), the problem of access to the children by anyone other than people approved by Richard, suggests that poisoning would be impossible to achieve.

One of the reasons that Richard lost support was that the Yorkists believed he had murdered his nephews. Even in a bloodthirsty age, the secret murder of children was considered to be a step too far. Nothing in Margaret's life suggests that she would have committed an act so unchristian.

A remarkably religious woman, even in a religious age, she did not show any obvious signs of guilt through the usual means of explicating sin in the 15th century – masses for the dead, pilgrimages, or requests to the Pope for indulgences. Although this is negative evidence, it certainly would support the view that Margaret's conscience was clear.

Nevertheless that is not to say that Margaret couldn't scheme, plan and, perhaps, deceive Buckingham. Her tenacity, determination, ability to wait patiently, and to seize an opportunity cannot be doubted – it is undoubtedly to these characteristics that Henry VII owes his throne.

Once she had achieved her objective of seeing her son crowned, Margaret seems, like Henry, to have eschewed violence as much as possible. There were genuine attempts by the Tudors to reconcile

Lancaster and York. Although, in a rather slippery fashion, Henry VII dated his reign to the day before Bosworth so that men who fought with Richard III could be branded as traitors, he never actually took advantage of this and made considerable efforts, as Edward IV had done initially, to work with both parties. Given the influence that Margaret had over him, we can conclude that, if she did not instigate this policy, she certainly agreed with it. She also took some of Richard's former servants into her own household.

The story was told by Bishop Fisher, her confessor and executor, that one of these former adherents of Richard, Sir Ralph Bigod, was held up to his fellow servants by her as an example of loyalty when he had objected to some of his colleagues denigrating his former master.

The exact level of influence that Margaret had over Henry has been debated. During her lifetime one of the Spanish ambassadors, Dr Pedro de Ayala, wrote home that the people with the most influence at Henry VII's court were first, Margaret, the mother of the King, then the Lord Chancellor, John Morton, followed by Reginald Bray. Bray was originally a servant of Margaret's second husband, Sir Henry Stafford, and had been a member of Margaret's entourage for many years. This would certainly support the contention that Margaret was extremely influential.

Polydor Virgil, the official historian of Henry VII's reign, writing after the King's death, claimed that Henry 'allotted a share (to Margaret) in most of his public and private resources.' He also describes her as 'a wise woman'.

Bernard Andre, who was tutor to Arthur, Prince of Wales, described Margaret as 'steadfast and more stable than the weakness in women suggests.'

Interests

If we can suppose that once Henry VII was safely on the throne, Margaret was free to indulge her own personal tastes, then we can conclude that her overriding concerns were religious, charitable and educational.

In the manner of the late 15th century, personal piety was very much wrapped up in prayers for the dead, rigorous fasting and prayer, veneration of relics, and support for religious foundations. Margaret, clearly of a conventional turn of mind, participated in all of these activities.

One of her earliest actions was the foundation of a chantry at Wimborne Minster, with an attached school, in memory of her parents. She also assigned property to Bourne Abbey where her Holland ancestors were buried.

Margaret Beaufort, like her Yorkist counterpart Cicely Neville, also known as 'my Lady, the King's mother', followed a stringent daily routine of prayer and devotion. She would rise at five in the morning to hear four or five masses before breakfast and her day was punctuated by private and public prayer. There were lighter moments, she enjoyed hunting and whilst eating her dinner, she would listen to 'merry tales', including Chaucer's Canterbury Tales and Boccaccio's saucy Decameron, but then after some light entertainment she would turn to more devotional literature.

Her accounts show significant charitable expenditure, particularly for orphans and children of poor women. According to Fisher in the eulogy preached after her death, which therefore may need to be taken with a slight pinch of salt as he is no doubt emphasising her best characteristics, she had a number of indigent people in her own household whom she would personally visit and treat if they were ill.

As early as 1476 when she was only in her early 30s Margaret had contributed to a crusade against the Turks which was being preached. In 1507, she also gave money to ransom Christians captured in the East.

Margaret appears to have had an extensive interest in literature, and not just in devotional works. In 1483 she commissioned a French romance called 'Blanchardyn and Englantine' from the printer, Caxton. The story, which is a romance, hinted at the hoped-for marriage between her son, Henry, and Elizabeth of York. It features a good deal of sighing over damsels in distress and other tropes of chivalric romance.

In 1489, she returned her copy of the book to Caxton and requested him to have it translated and printed. A later work also printed for Lady Margaret, in conjunction with her daughter-in-law Queen Elizabeth, was an edition of the 'Fifteen Ohs', which were prayers attributed to St Bridget of Sweden.

Margaret also patronised Wynkyn de Worde who succeeded Caxton in his printing shop. In 1494, de Worde published the devotional work 'Scala Perfectionis', referring to Margaret in the dedication. This text was particularly appreciated by the Carthusian and Bridgettine Orders which Margaret supported.

Book purchases were made both at home and abroad. She commissioned Ingelbert de Rouen to purchase books for her in Paris and also to print the Hereford Breviary. He later sold her old Mass books, printed on vellum. In order to keep up with all the books she had, she employed a couple of her servants to undertake bookbinding and illumination.

Although we have no knowledge of the details of Margaret's education, she was sufficiently proficient to translate from French into English. She regretted her lack of facility with Latin but seems to have tried to study it in later years.

Her most complex work of translation was of the fourth book of Thomas a Kempis' *'Imitation of Christ'*. This book, still widely read today, was one of the most influential works of the late Middle Ages. It concentrates on personal piety and is applicable to lay people as well as clerics. Margaret worked on the fourth book herself, having commissioned a Cambridge Fellow to undertake the first three chapters from Latin. The combined translation was published in 1504, and then reissued about 15 years later. This probably makes Margaret the first woman in England to publish her work, pre-dating the work of Margaret Roper and later Margaret's granddaughter-in-law, Katherine Parr.

Chapter 14: Appearance and Possessions

The only certain knowledge we have of Margaret's physical appearance is the information that she was of slight stature. This was particularly noted in her traumatic childbirth. Her funeral effigy, which was probably taken from a death mask, shows a thin woman with high cheekbones, a hooked nose and drawn cheeks. The pictures labelled as likenesses of her, none of which date from her lifetime, are sufficiently like the funeral effigy to suggest that they are copies of an original. There is another picture, alleged to be of her as a young woman, but we would question it, as the headdress style dates to the early 1500s, when Margaret was in her sixties.

Henry VII was a thin man and is recorded to have been blonde with grey eyes. Given that the majority of the English Royal family was fair and blue-eyed, it certainly seems possible that Henry inherited these traits from his mother, especially as his father was of mixed Welsh and French descent.

Of course, her slight figure could have been partially the result of the regular fasting and generally abstemious life-style she followed. She was certainly able to have a dig at fatter women. When she was presented with a pair of gloves from Henry VII's arch-enemy, Margaret of York, Dowager Duchess of Burgundy, she found them too large. She commented that the ladies of Europe obviously had *'great personages'* to match their *'great states.'*

The pictures that we have of Margaret show her soberly garbed in black with a widow's coif, however black was not necessarily just the colour of mourning but was one of most expensive fabrics available. The inventory after her death shows that she also had a number of scarlet gowns and the black was often decorated with ermines.

Another indicator of wealth and status that Margaret enjoyed were tapestries. Tapestries were some of the most valuable items in Tudor England. A group, known as a *'chamber'* of tapestries, would be hung in a room narrating a story. They would then be moved with the owner to different houses.

Margaret's tapestries included ones of the Labours of Hercules (later sold to Thomas Howard, Earl of Surrey for £40) and other themes of classical antiquity, as well as biblical stories. All of her tapestries and hangings were liberally bedecked with Beaufort portcullises and red roses. Her personal items included ivory combs, purses, cramp rings, little silver pots for cosmetics and medicines, a golden goblet with a portcullis, silver candlesticks and spoons. As a nod to her advancing age she had two pairs of gold rimmed spectacles.

Margaret left boxes of jewels, including pearls, rubies, sapphires, Garter devices and, of course, a number of religious items and reliquaries.   Her chapel was filled with images of saints – St Mary Magdalen, St John the Baptist, St George, St Margaret, St Anne, Peter, and St Anthony.   She fasted regularly, particularly in honour of her favourite saints.   Saint Catherine was of special interest to Margaret as a patron of scholars.   Margaret's devotion to the cult of the Name of Jesus explains the frequent use of the symbol IHS, representing His name, in many of the items and buildings associated with her.

Like all royalty and nobles of the period Margaret and her son enjoyed hunting.   Margaret gave strict orders that her parks at Collyweston and Madeley in Staffordshire should be kept full of stock for the King's pleasure.

At her death her assets were valued at £14,724.

Chapter 15: Patron of Learning

Lady Margaret's longest lasting achievement is probably her establishment of two Cambridge Colleges.   University Colleges were foundations that brought together both monks and secular priests to study, debate and, most importantly, pray for the souls of their benefactors.

Margaret was not the first royal patron of Colleges at Oxford or Cambridge or even the first woman to support the universities. Previous noble women had been closely involved with both universities – Lady Elizabeth de Clare in the foundation of Clare College Cambridge and Marie de Vallance, Countess of Pembroke, in that of the eponymous College at Oxford.   More recently the Lancastrian and Yorkist Queens,

Marguerite of Anjou, Elizabeth Woodville and Anne Neville, had contributed to Queens' College, Cambridge.

Her association with the universities which were largely devoted to the training of theologians, the vast majority of whom took holy orders, seems to have begun in the mid-1490s. In 1494 she requested Oxford to release one of its fellows, Maurice Westbury, to enter her household to teach the young men in her wardship – these pupils may have included Sir Nicholas Vaux and his stepson, and later brother-in-law, Sir Thomas Parr.

In 1494 there are also records of her lending money to scholars and maintaining at least two.

Initially Margaret showed an interest in both Oxford and Cambridge. She endowed a professional Lectureship of Divinity at both universities, both of which continue to this day, under the name the Lady Margaret Professorship.

Originally the lectureships were to be maintained out of the lands granted by Margaret and Henry VII to their planned chantry at St George's, Windsor, however their interest in St George's declined as plans for a Royal mausoleum were transferred to Westminster Abbey. The grants given to Westminster were earmarked to provide funds for the professorships.

In a break with tradition, however, the University lectureships were given their own legal personae. The result of this was that the Universities would be able to sue the Westminster foundation should it fail to provide the agreed emoluments. Until these arrangements were finalised, Margaret supported the lectureships from her own pocket.

In 1498 the lecturers were Dr Smyth at Cambridge and Dr Wills at Oxford. Following the formal inauguration of the positions, the first

Lady Margaret Professor at Cambridge was her confessor and close associate, John Fisher. Fisher influenced Margaret from the moment they met and he worked closely with her in her schemes for Cambridge. He was appointed Bishop of Rochester in 1504 with Henry VII asking his mother's confirmation that she was happy for him to be offered the appointment. The Oxford Lecturer was Dr John Roper. Each of these lecturers was to give an hour's lecture every day when lectures customarily took place during the University terms.

In addition to the lectureships, Margaret also founded a University Preachership at Cambridge. The preacher, who should preferably be a Doctor of Theology, was to be chosen every three years by the Chancellor of the University. Ideally he was also to be a Fellow of one of the Colleges. His job was to preach six sermons a year, including an annual one at St Paul's Cross. Of course there are no free lunches or lectures and the quid pro quo was that the souls of Margaret, her husbands, ancestors and descendants were all to be prayed for.

By the end of the century, her main focus was on Cambridge. This is probably because her new confessor, John Fisher, was a Cambridge man.

Margaret began her patronage of Cambridge with Jesus College. Along with a number of other nobles and courtiers, she gave it financial support and it was with one of its fellows, Dr William Atkinson, that she undertook her translation of the 'Imitation of Christ'.

She also showed an interest in Queens' College and requested that it appoint John Fisher as its President. She helped with its funding by encouraging her former ward, Edward Stafford, 3rd Duke of Buckingham, to endow it with land. It was to Queens' that the humanist, Desidirius Erasmus, first went when he lived in England between 1511 and 1514.

Margaret's major contribution, though was to Christ's College Cambridge. It had already been founded in 1439 under the name of

God's House. Its first founder was a London rector named William Bingham who wished to create a College to train masters to teach in the grammar schools.

As part of Henry VI's organisation of the King's College buildings, God's House was given a new site but it did not have a sufficient endowment to fulfil its mission effectively. Nevertheless this association with the Lancastrian monarchy was a good opportunity for Margaret to take over the project.

With the possible exception of Lady Elizabeth de Clare, Margaret took the most personal interest in her colleges of all of royal founders and was closely involved in instituting the rules and regulations by which they were to be managed.

In 1504 plans began to be put together for organising the financial affairs of the new College. On 1st May 1505 Henry VII granted letters patent for Margaret to *augment, establish and finish the college'* of God's House. Margaret received a papal bull in August 1505 confirming that she had established and augmented the College for the study of theology and the liberal sciences.

The current incumbents were permitted to transfer to the new College which was intended to house a maximum of 60 scholars. The original purpose of the College, training of masters in grammar teaching, was to remain. In recognition of its status as the College founded by a member of the royal family, it had the privilege of being exempt from visitation by the local Bishop.

Margaret took a personal interest in the arrangements. She purchased a vicarage for the College's vicar and arranged for it to be extended with extra rooms, new chimneys, windows and doors.

The College statutes were finalised in 1506 and she personally began one copy by writing in her own hand at the top of the page 'Nos Margarita' (We, Margaret).

Margaret anticipated visiting her College frequently and rooms were set aside for her, although how often she stayed there is not recorded. It is probable that she was there in late 1506 for the opening of the College and in the following year a local woman was given a tip for bringing her a cake. There is an account of her, whilst visiting the College, calling out of the window to one of the masters who was beating a student (a regular occurrence). Margaret exhorted him to do it 'lente, lente' (gently).

As well as cash from endowments granted by Margaret, some of the building materials for the College came directly from Margaret's lands. Eighty-six loads of timber came from Bourne and significant amounts from Collyweston; both properties were within 50 miles of Cambridge. She also paid for books for the College and gave it ceremonial plate. Some 39 books are listed in the inventory of 1639 as having been donated by her, however there is no contemporary evidence as to exactly which they were.

The curriculum was to include logic and philosophy to be studied by 12 Fellows and 47 Scholars. Throughout her life Margaret was to remain responsible for appointing the Master and the Fellows, half of whom would be chosen from the northern counties of England. Concerned about the health of her students, she arranged for the Manor at Malton to be available in times of plague – a frequent occurrence in the wet and boggy fens of Cambridgeshire.

As noted before, however, the inmates of the College were expected to provide something in return. They were to pray for Margaret herself, her husband Edmund Tudor, Earl of Richmond, her parents and other ancestors, the late Queen Elizabeth of York, for the original founder of God's House, William Bingham and for Henry VI.

Margaret visited Cambridge in June 1505 and is recorded as having been rowed down the River Cam to listen to disputations at the Schools. In 1507 she was there with Henry VII and her grandson, Arthur, Prince of Wales, at the University Commencement in the Greyfriars Church.

To give an indication of the cost of all of these foundations, Henry VII, in total, contributed £6, 850 to Cambridge, which was about twice the value of Margaret's estates.

Once Christ's College was well in hand and the souls of the dead were being busily prayed for, John Fisher suggested a new project to Margaret: the re-foundation of the Hospital of St John the Evangelist. By 1505 this hospital had decayed to the extent that there were only three brothers left. Margaret began to consider this and how best to finance it.

As Margaret's health begun to fail from 1505, she was occupied with changing and updating her will regularly. It was customary in the period for nobles to regularly review their wills, so her annual updates were not particularly morbid. She had been putting aside money since 1472 into a trust to fulfil her testamentary requirements. In February 1509 a new schedule was drawn up which outlined the bequests to Christ's College and her other charitable works, with the exception of St John's.

St John's was dealt with in a separate document in the following month. It was initially unclear whether the monies she had set aside in her trust to deal with her testamentary requirements could be used for St John's College and by the time of her death in 1509 no definite arrangements had been made. In November 1512, a month after her will was proved, it was decided that the trust monies could be so used until the College should be completed, after which her estate was to pass to her heir, her grandson Henry VIII.

Perhaps not surprisingly the College's view of when it would be completed turned out to be rather different from that of the King and there were a number of financial disputes between Margaret's executors, of whom Bishop Fisher was chief, and Henry VIII.

Fisher's determination to create St John's in accordance with his vision and that of Margaret caused a number of disputes with Henry VIII – it is perhaps in the knowledge of this that we can see the seeds of dislike and perhaps resentment that would finally come to fruition in the execution of Fisher in 1535 for defying the King in the matter of the Royal supremacy. There is a note from Fisher that disputes over the will had made Henry *'a very heavy Lord against me'*.

Another obstacle was the Bishop of Ely (Margaret's stepson) who, chagrined at being removed from his visitation rights at Christ's College, was insisting that, before he would give consent for St John's Hospital to be translated into the new College, he must be given rights of nomination of the Fellows.

The College was finally opened on 29 July 1516 with the full complement of 31 Fellows by 1524 in which year the target of £300 income per annum had been achieved. The scholars were to pray for Margaret and her parents, Henry VII, Henry VIII as well as her Lancastrian cousin, Henry VI, his wife Marguerite of Anjou and their son, Edward of Lancaster, Prince of Wales.

The great gateway of St John's College reflects its debt to Margaret. Her arms are everywhere: the crowned Rose, the Beaufort portcullis and daisy flowers in a nod to her name, are scattered into the stonework. Margaret is remembered every day in the grace recited after dinner in Hall.

St John's Cambridge was to become one of the Colleges at the forefront of the New Learning revolution of the 1520s and 30s. Many of the alumni of the College were leaders of the Protestant Reformation in England – Roger Ascham, William Cecil, John Cheke. It seems unlikely that Margaret would have approved of the evangelical movement, however in her way she did attempt to reform some of the problems of the mediaeval church by improving standards of training and education.

Chapter 16: Following the Footsteps of Margaret Beaufort

Lady Margaret was a great heiress, and her lands stretched across the Southern and Midland counties of England. As a married woman, she lived in Wales and the North of England, and travelled extensively around the country as she visited her different homes and the royal court.

The numbers in the article below correspond to those on the map which follows.

*

Lady Margaret was born in her mother's castle of Bletsoe (1) in Bedfordshire. Bletsoe is a small hamlet with little to identify it as being the location of a castle. The only clue that there was ever a castle here, is in the name Castle Lane. Nothing remains of the building, with the possible exception of some barns that may date from the period. Opposite the castle's former location is St Andrew's Church, which dates from the 13th century and would have been known to Margaret, who paid for some renovations in later life.

Margaret's father died about a year after her birth and was buried in Wimborne Minster (2), Dorset. Her mother, however, lived for another 40 years before joining him there. Wimborne is a fascinating church with an important library of ancient books, as well as the tombs of Margaret's parents, the Duke and Duchess of Somerset, and no less a personage than King Ethelred, brother of Alfred the Great.

In 1497 Margaret was granted permission by Letters Patent from Henry VII, to found a chantry staffed by a single chaplain at Wimborne.

She was given a licence to appropriate land to the value of £10 per annum to support the chaplain. Following her death, Henry VIII, on 7 August 1509 confirmed the grant and gave additional lands to provide a further £6.

The chaplain was to pray for the souls of Margaret, her parents and other ancestors, and all the faithful departed. In addition to his duties as chaplain the first incumbent, Richard Hodgekynnes, was required to teach grammar as it was taught at Eton and Winchester. A Requiem Mass was to be so held each year on 29th July, the anniversary of the death of her husband, Thomas Stanley, Earl of Derby There are other detailed instructions for the conduct of the bequest and the requirements for the chaplain.

The Chantry was suppressed following the Dissolution, but the school was re-founded by Margaret's great-granddaughter, Elizabeth I, and is still extant as Queen Elizabeth's School, Wimborne, closely attached to the Minster.

Despite being made a ward of the Earl of Suffolk, in anticipation of her marriage to his son John, it seems that Margaret probably stayed in her mother's home rather than living with the Suffolks. She spent the majority of her time at the Dowager Duchess' property, Maxey Castle (3). Not far from Bletsoe, Maxey was then in the Soke of Peterborough but is now considered to be in Cambridgeshire. The site of this castle, which was licensed for crenellation in 1374, is a scheduled ancient monument, although there is little to be seen.

Margaret would have lived there with her half-siblings from her mother's first marriage, the St Johns, and the step-siblings she acquired on her mother's third marriage to Lionel, Lord Welles. Also in the household were the children that her mother and Lord Welles had and probably her father's illegitimate daughter, Tacine.

Not long after Margaret's marriage to Edmund Tudor, Earl of Richmond, which took place at the Bishop's Palace in Llandyfai (Lamphey) (4), Pembrokeshire, she and her new husband set up home in Pembroke Castle (5), in the far west of Wales. Margaret presumably believed that she would spend her life there as mistress of a great household, visiting other manors and castles within the honour of Richmond. Sadly, it was not to be. Within a year of their marriage Edmund died, after being captured and imprisoned in Carmarthen Castle, by Sir William Herbert, a Yorkist adherent.

In April 1457 the widowed Margaret remarried. Her second husband, who was around 15 years older than her, was Sir Henry Stafford, son of Humphrey, 1st Duke of Buckingham. The marriage took place at the Buckingham seat of Maxstoke Castle(6) in Warwickshire. The castle and enormous mediaeval construction still exists and is lived in by a family which has owned it since the Civil War. It is occasionally open to the public.

Margaret was a considerable heiress, even though, on her father's death, the title of Duke of Somerset had been inherited by her uncle Edmund. She and Stafford set up home first at Bourne Castle (7) in Lincolnshire, and then later at Woking (8) in Surrey. There is no trace of their home at Bourne, other than a watercourse in the town which was once part of the moat. By the 1520s the castle had fallen into disrepair.

Working Palace lay off what is now the Old Woking Road in Surrey, with the River Wey as its southern boundary. The first record of a manor house there dates from 1272, and it was part of the inheritance of Lady Margaret's grandmother, Lady Margaret Holland, Countess of Somerset and then Duchess of Clarence. Woking appears to have been Margaret's preferred home until it was taken from her, not without some objection,, by Henry VII in 1503. Henry VIII also liked the Palace and extended it significantly between 1515 and 1543. It was used by Elizabeth I but then granted by James I to one of his courtiers, Edward Zouche (d. 1634). Zouche used some of the materials from the Palace to build a new house. There is an archaeological dig at Woking Palace which is sometimes open to the public.

It was from Woking that Henry Stafford departed to join the Yorkists at the 2nd Battle of Barnet which took place on 14 April 1471. Stafford sustained wounds that probably killed him. He was buried later that year at Holy Trinity Church (9), Pleshey, Essex, on the outskirts of Chelmsford.

Holy Trinity Church was founded by Thomas of Woodstock, Duke of Gloucester, ancestor of the Stafford Dukes of Buckingham. Henry Stafford's father had been laid to rest there after his death fighting for Lancaster at the Battle of Towton. Nine years after Henry's death, his mother, Anne Neville, Duchess of Buckingham, was also buried there. The Buckingham tombs can still be seen.

Widowed for a second time, Margaret lost no time in selecting another husband. This time she would have been completely free to choose herself, and her selection fell on Thomas, Lord Stanley. Stanley was a great magnate in the North West of England, as well as being hereditary King of Man. The main Stanley seats were at Knowsley (10) and Lathom (11) in Lancashire. Knowsley was replaced during the 18th century but is still the seat of the Earls of Derby and is occasionally open to the public. There is no trace remaining of Lathom.

Margaret divided her time mainly between these Lancashire properties and the court, where she was frequently in attendance on Queen Elizabeth Woodville and later, on Queen Anne Neville. Following the failed rebellion of Margaret's nephew-by-marriage, the 2nd Duke of Buckingham, she was largely confined to the Stanley estates in

Lancashire, more or less under house arrest. Her own estates were confiscated and re-granted to her husband.

This all changed in 1485 when Henry VII won the throne at the Battle of Bosworth. One of his first actions was to grant Margaret the Palace of Coldharbour (12) in London. Like most of the great London palaces, Coldharbour has completely disappeared. It was located not far from where Cannon Street station is today.

Henry also granted her extensive estates on the Northamptonshire/Lincolnshire border at Collyweston (13). Collyweston is in the Welland Valley at the edge of Rutland. The Manor house was built in the early 15th century by Sir William Porter and was later sold to Ralph, Lord Cromwell. It is not clear how it came into the hands of the Crown, but it was granted to Margaret not long after Henry's victory at Bosworth. She undertook considerable works there, developing a sumptuous country house.

It continued in royal use, with Henry Fitzroy, Duke of Richmond, Henry VIII's illegitimate son, living there. After Henry VIII's death it was one of the properties assigned to his daughter, Elizabeth. Nothing remains of the palace, apart from a dovecote, together with some alterations she made to the parish church. There is a sundial which is said to date from the old palace but it is probably 18th century in origin.

Margaret's most lasting contribution to architecture, as well as learning, was the re-founding of two somewhat impoverished Cambridge Colleges. The first, originally known as God's House, and founded by Henry VI, was refounded by her as Christ's College (14). She endowed it with significant revenues and it remains her greatest monument. In her will she also allocated money for the founding of a second college St John's, which was to replace the impecunious St John's Hospital. Both of Margaret's Cambridge Colleges are liberally festooned with her graphic badges – the Beaufort portcullis, the Yale of Kendal and the Roses of Lancaster.

Margaret did not long survive her son, Henry VII, and in June 1509, she was buried in Westminster Abbey (15). The tomb under which she lies was commissioned in 1511 by her grandson, Henry VIII, from the renowned Italian sculptor Pietro Torregiano, who had also undertaken the works on the tomb of Henry VII and Elizabeth of York.

The epitaph on her tomb was written by Erasmus:

'Margaret of Richmond, mother of Henry VII, grandmother of Henry VIII, who gave a salary to three monks of this convent and founded a grammar school at Wimborne, and to a preacher throughout England, and to two interpreters of Scripture, one at Oxford, the other at Cambridge, where she likewise founded two colleges, one to Christ, and the other to St John, his disciple. Died A.D.1509, III Kalends of July [29 June]'"

The list overleaf corresponds to the map which follows of places Margaret Beaufort would have known.

Key to Map

1. Bletsoe Castle, Bedfordshire
2. Wimborne Minster, Dorset
3. Maxey Castle, Cambridgeshire
4. Bishop's Palace Llandyfai (Lamphey), Pembrokeshire
5. Pembroke Castle, Pembrokeshire
6. Maxstoke Castle, Warwickshire
7. Bourne, Lincolnshire
8. Woking, Surrey
9. Holy Trinity Church, Pleshey, Essex
10. Knowsley, Merseyside
11. Lathom Castle, Lancashire
12. Coldharbour Palace, London
13. Collyweston Palace, Northamptonshire
14. Christ Church College, Cambridge
15. Westminster Abbey, London

Map

Chapter 17: Two Book Reviews

There is quite a range of books about the Wars of the Roses, in which Margaret Beaufort played such a significant part. Two that we have reviewed are: Dan Jones' *'The Hollow Crown'* and *'Jasper Tudor: Dynasty Maker'* by Terry Breverton.

The Hollow Crown

Author: Dan Jones

Publisher: Faber & Faber

In a nutshell A panoramic sweep through English History from the marriage of Henry V in 1420, to the death of Margaret Plantagenet, Countess of Salisbury in 1541. A really thorough analysis, for experts and newcomers alike – fast-moving but with enormous amounts of detail packed into every paragraph.

It is generally not hard to tell whether a writer's sympathies lie with Lancaster or York, but in the case of *The Hollow Crown*, Jones is even-handed and judicious throughout. His devastating critique of Henry VI as entirely unfit for the inheritance left him by that Plantagenet hero, Henry V, is matched by his incisive portrait of Richard, Duke of York, as self-important, partisan and as lacking in political finesse as Queen Marguerite.

The political theory that underlies the whole work, is that, in the late Middle Ages having a King of legitimate royal descent was not enough for the realm to function effectively. If the character of the man wearing the Crown was not sufficiently robust, and he failed to wield his power effectively, there was no way of filling the vacuum.

During the minority of Henry VI, his uncles and the other magnates held the realm together reasonably successfully, but there was no prescription for the ills that followed from an adult King who could not step up to his responsibilities. Yet, the lords were hamstrung in reacting to the situation. Henry was not a tyrant – rather he was a gentle and kindly man, so there was no excuse for his overthrow. Attempts by others to manage the kingdom on Henry's behalf were resented and feared by both the nobles excluded from the King's inner circle, and the public at large. Jones rehabilitates William de la Pole, Earl of Suffolk, who is often vilified, but, initially, at least, tried to keep Henry's rule on track.

As royal authority disintegrated in the 1440s and 1450s, there was growing discontent, and personal feuds between members of the nobility began to get out of hand – a situation not helped by Henry's wife, Marguerite of Anjou. It is hard not to admire some aspects of Marguerite's character as Jones presents her – she was phenomenally brave, determined and resolute in her attempts to protect the throne for her husband and son, but she was violently partisan, and, rather than rising above Court rivalries, she made the situation far worse.

Jones moves smoothly through the numerous battles that took place up and down the land, and keeps the reader on top of the dizzying changes of loyalties that characterised the period as the Crown became a plaything of the man with the biggest army. It is with a sense of relief, that must echo that of the population of 1471, that we read of the triumph of Edward IV at Tewkesbury, bringing a King to the throne who had something of the skill, tenacity and strategic brilliance of Henry V: a man whom the vast majority of Lancastrians were willing to accept as King, with Edward of Lancaster dead. The murder of Henry VI was skated over by most people as a little local difficulty.

But knocking an old and incompetent man on the head was one thing – usurping the throne of a twelve year old boy was quite another. Jones shows clearly how the usurpation of Richard III undermined all of the good work done by Edward IV. Richard may have had good instincts in how he wanted to rule, but nothing could undo the damage of his grab for the throne. Jones is no revisionist – it is perfectly plain to him that Richard had his nephews murdered. This one act, against all odds, united the remnants of Lancaster, with the supporters of Edward IV, and brought the obscure Henry Tudor, Earl of Richmond, to the throne.

Unlike most historians, Jones does not bring the Wars to a close in 1485, or 1487 with Henry VII's victory at Stoke. He goes on to show how the lingering suspicion, the fear that any plausible rogue with an army could emulate the success of Henry in overthrowing an anointed monarch, slowly poisoned Henry's reign and led to the imprisonment and execution of almost anyone with a vague claim to the throne.

A new era appeared to dawn in 1509, with the accession of Henry VIII, heir to both Lancaster and York, but still the old fears ran deep. After an early attempt to bring the extended royal family together to turn the nobility's minds towards that perennial delight, war with France, dissensions from Henry's policies began to emerge. Nevertheless, Jones contends, the main focus was no longer the old one of York versus Lancaster, but, increasingly, families were divided between Catholic and Protestant. The final purge of possible claimants to the throne in 1538 – 41, when Montague, Exeter and the aged Countess of Salisbury were executed, was the last effusion of Plantagenet blood.

The Hollow Crown demands concentration – a huge amount of ground is covered – but it is well worth it. I can promise you will not be bored for a moment!

Jasper Tudor: Dynasty Maker

Author: Terry Breverton

Publisher: Amberley Publishing

In a nutshell: A fantastically detailed look at the Wars of the Roses in the context of a man who never wavered in his allegiance, and whose tenacity ensured the ultimate triumph of Henry Tudor.

Terry Breverton is the author of a wide range of books with topics as diverse as pirates, herbals and the First World War. His specialism, however, is Welsh topics, and his comprehensive research into the Welsh experience of the Wars of the Roses, and the reaction of Wales to calls from both Lancastrian and Yorkist Kings gives a whole new perspective to the conflict. Breverton concentrates on the life of Jasper Tudor, second son of Queen Catherine de Valois by her second husband, Owain Tudor. Jasper was one of the few men present at both the opening battle of the War – St Albans in 1455 – and the final confrontation at Stoke in 1487.

Jasper, like his older brother, Edmund, received recognition and a generous endowment from his half-brother, Henry VI. Breverton looks at Jasper's early career and discovers that, during the 1440s and 1450s, far from being a blind partisan of Henry's inept government, he was on good terms with Richard of York, and sought to support York's attempts to improve it. It was not until the Yorkists took up arms against the King that Jasper firmly committed himself to fight for his half-brother.

Breverton has undertaken extensive research into the government offices and landholdings in Wales, and how they changed hands over the course of the wars – he identifies three great power bases – Jasper's own, which he continued to control to a degree until the defeat of the Lancasatrians at Tewkesbury in 1571; that of William Herbert (or Gwilym Du, '*Black William*', in his native Welsh) and that of Rhys ap Thomas. Herbert was originally part of Jasper's own affinity, but shifted his allegiance to Edward IV, and was rewarded with Jasper's earldom of Pembroke. He also became the guardian of Jasper's nephew, Henry Tudor. Even more than in England, the personally loyalty of men to their lord affected their willingness to fight for the lord's chosen side. Nowhere is this more clearly shown than in the reaction of Wales to the revolt of the Duke of Buckingham against Richard III in 1483.

Buckingham, although he had been granted wide-ranging powers in the country, had little or no personal following among the Welsh, who largely ignored the uprising. It was a different story when Jasper and Henry Tudor arrived in 1485 – the Herberts, who were Yorkists, made no attempt to prevent his march, Rhys ap Thomas, who had been a Yorkist actively supported him, and the northern counties of Denbighshire and Flintshire, under the leadership of the Stanleys, also fell in behind the Red Dragon banner.

Breverton makes use of a wide range of Welsh bardic and literary sources – which, although less well known, are not necessarily more, or less accurate, than the English sources despite often being written in poetic style, rather than as factual accounts. The language used in them illustrates pent up anger in Wales against the conquest of the country and the vicious penal laws enacted against Owain Glyndwr at the turn of the fifteenth century. The prophesies of a Welshman who would free them from the Saxon yoke was a dream that many could follow. Had Henry and Jasper landed in England they would have been far less likely to gather the number of troops they did before crossing the border.

Following the victory at Bosworth, for which Henry VII could thank Jasper, and that other Lancastrian stalwart, the Earl of Oxford, Jasper was the only man granted a dukedom and was showered with land (including Sudeley Castle) and offices from his grateful nephew. He was also granted a wife, connected to the family of Edward IV. Katherine Woodville, widow of the Duke of Buckingham, was in her late twenties, compared with Jasper's fifty-four, but the fact that she was aunt to Elizabeth of York, whom Henry had vowed to marry, strengthened the relationship between the formerly warring factions. At no time does Breverton speculate on Jasper's private life (fifty-four being extremely old for a noble to marry for the first time in the fifteenth century). He mentions the theory that Jasper had been in love with his sister-in-law, Margaret Beaufort, but suggests that the most likely reason is that the Wars of the Roses had begun before a suitable bride had been found, and that Jasper had not had time subsequently to marry. Marriage to Katherine was also a way of providing Jasper with a very fine income as the Duchess' dower rights (confiscated by Richard III) were returned.

Breverton's interpretations of Jasper's character are limited to observations where he believes he has direct evidence – he contends that Jasper was of a conciliatory nature and encouraged Henry VII to seek reconciliation with the Yorkists rather than another round of blood-letting, citing the easy terms given by Jasper to the adherents of Francis Lovell's rather lack-lustre rebellion in early 1486.

Jasper's final years as Henry's most trusted advisor (except for Margaret Beaufort) are covered – including his final military command –

an expedition into France that ended with a peace treaty. He also acted as deputy for the infant Arthur, Prince of Wales in the Council of Wales, based at Ludlow.

I really enjoyed this book – the wealth of detail, the Welsh perspective – so little considered elsewhere – and, in good Welsh fashion the minutiae of familial relationships between the various men of Jasper's affinity. I have only one negative comment – the book is long, and there is very frequent repetition of the same fact, even the same sentence over several pages. A good edit would remove these annoyances, and make the narrative flow more tightly.

Bibliography

Ballard, George, and Ruth Perry, *Memoirs of Several Ladies of Great Britain: Who Have Been Celebrated for Their Writings or Skill in the Learned Languages, Arts, and Sciences* (Detroit: Wayne State University Press, 1985)

Breverton, Terry, *Jasper Tudor: Dynasty Maker*, 1st edn (Gloucestershire: Amberley Publishing, 2015)

Buck, Sir George, *The History of the Life and Reign of King Richard the Third*, ed. by Arthur Noel Kincaid (London, 1647)

Christ's College, Cambridge https://www.christs.cam.ac.uk/

De Lisle, Leanda, *Tudor: The Family Story* (United Kingdom: Chatto & Windus, 2013)

Gristwood, Sarah, *Blood Sisters: The Women Behind the Wars of the Roses*. Kindle (HarperPress, 2013)

Http://www.british-history.ac.uk/rchme/northants/vol1/pp29-32 [accessed 7 December 2015]

Jones, Dan, *The Hollow Crown: The Wars of the Roses and the Rise of The Tudors*, 1st edn (United Kingdom: Faber & Faber Non-Fiction, 2014)

Jones, Michael K, and Malcolm G Underwood, *The King's Mother: Lady Margaret Beaufort, Countess of Richmond and Derby*, 1st edn (New York: Cambridge University Press, Cambridge, 1991)

Norton, Elizabeth, *Margaret Beaufort: The Mother of the Tudor Dynasty* (United Kingdom: Amberley Publishing, 2010)

Skidmore, Chris, *Bosworth: The Birth of the Tudors*, 1st edn (London: W&N, 2014)

'St   John's   College,   '   Cambridge'
<http://www.joh.cam.ac.uk/college-history>

www.tudortimes.co.uk

Printed in Great Britain
by Amazon